true
IMAGES
DEVOTIONAL

Perfect companion to the **True Images Bible**

90 DAILY
DEVOTIONS
FOR
TEEN GIRLS

true
IMAGES
DEVOTIONAL

Karen Moore

ZONDERVAN®

ZONDERVAN.com/
AUTHORTRACKER
follow your favorite authors

ZONDERVAN

True Images Devotional: Revised
Copyright © 2005 by The Livingstone Corporation
Copyright © 2012 by Karen Moore

This title is also available as a Zondervan ebook.
Visit www.zondervan.com/ebooks.

Requests for information should be addressed to:

Zondervan, 5300 Patterson SW, Grand Rapids, Michigan 49530

Library of Congress Cataloging-in-Publication Data
CIP Applied for: ISBN 978-0-310-72606-7

Contents

bless the stress and
MOVE ON!

A LITTLE ANXIETY IS A GOOD THING! It pushes you to study harder, to practice more of the things you do well, or to get more involved in good causes. When you worry a little about something, it shows you care about the outcome.

But the key is "a little." Let anxiety become the ruler of your life, the king of your domain, the nagging voice that feeds your nightmares, and you'll find yourself on shaky ground. That kind of stress just makes you a mess.

Martin Luther suggested it would be a good idea to simply "pray and let God worry." He had the right idea. Do pray. Talk things through with God and let him remind you who defines your worth. *He* does. Not school or work or scholarships or even acts of service. Just God.

If you're walking around with so much stress you can't function well, then you need to seek out earthly help too. Parents, teachers, friends, and counselors can all make a difference if you let them.

Give up the kind of stress that ruins your days, and give in to getting the right kind of help when you need it.

SCRIPTURE

Humble yourselves, therefore, under God's mighty hand, that he may lift you up in due time. Cast all your anxiety on him because he cares for you.

1 Peter 5:6 – 7

TALK WITH GOD

Lord, I am such a worrywart. I keep thinking I can just let things go, but I don't. Please help me to remember I'm not alone. I have you, and I have others who care about me too. Today, I put all my worries in your hands. Thank you, Lord. Amen.

what are you THINKING?

IS THE GLASS HALF EMPTY OR HALF FULL? Are you sure you're going to win today or sure something will go wrong? Like it or not, your attitude influences the way you experience the world.

From champion athletes and billionaire businesspeople to your own school's star quarterback and valedictorian, successful people nearly always owe part of their success to a positive attitude. They believe that good things will happen to them, so good things often do happen.

In his letter to the Ephesians, Paul reminded believers how important their attitude was. Ephesians 4:22–23 says that you are "to put off your old self, which is being corrupted by its deceitful desires [and] to be made new in the attitude of your minds."

In other words, you have control over how you choose to see things. You can look for positive ways to grow through the bad stuff, and then you can really hold on to what you know of the good stuff. It's your choice.

Changing your mind requires one thing, though. You have to be willing to be honest with yourself, your family, and your friends. God designed you to be unique and special just as you are. That's why he gave you a mind of your own and the ability to make choices.

Go on, then. Change things up a bit and make it a great day!

SCRIPTURE

I can do all [things] through him who gives me strength. *Philippians 4:13*

TALK WITH GOD

Lord, I know that my attitude isn't always the best. In fact, I seem to totally forget sometimes that the way I think has anything to do with me. Help me to look for the good things you have planned for me each and every day. Amen.

who's in CHARGE here?

YOU OBEY THE RULES AT HOME, listen to your parents, and do your best to stay within the guidelines, but now that you're getting older and more responsible, you realize that obedience doesn't really end there. Someone is always in charge, and it seldom feels like it's you.

The best way to learn how to be a leader or even a good follower is to learn to respect those in authority. Imagine that you just got your driver's license and went out on the road, only to discover that everyone followed their own rules. People went through red lights, turned without signaling, and drove at any speed. Whatever anyone felt like doing was okay, except that everyone was in danger of being hurt all the time. Would you want to drive on that road?

Having rules and people who enforce them is indeed important when you're driving. And just like cops on the road, parents, teachers, and others who have authority over you deserve your respect because they're trying to help keep you happy and safe as you enjoy everything around you. And since God is the ultimate authority, we all look to him for guidance both personally and in community with others. When everything works together, having someone in charge isn't bad after all.

SCRIPTURE

Jesus came to [his disciples] and said, "All authority in heaven and on earth has been given to me."

Matthew 28:18

TALK WITH GOD

Lord, sometimes people in authority can be scary. They sometimes abuse their power or neglect their responsibilities to those under them. I know we all need help and guidance, so I pray for everyone today who has authority over someone else, that they'll be wise and caring. Amen.

what is BEAUTY?

THE PERSON WHO SAID "beauty is in the eye of the beholder" got it right. After all, everybody has a different way of seeing things and deciding if they're beautiful or not. For example, you might look at a painting and think it's amazing. But other people might miss the point the artist was making and think the painting is ugly.

Just like people can misjudge a painting, the world often defines beauty only by surface appearances. Maybe you struggle with the idea of beauty presented in magazine styles and on prom queens, but that is beauty in its most shallow form. Real beauty radiates from the heart. Unlike surface beauty, this inner beauty has everything to do with who you really are. When you shine the light of God's love on your friends and family, on people you meet and classmates that others ignore, your innate beauty comes through, and the message of the Artist who created you is harder to miss. You're beautiful, pure and simple!

If you're going to work on your own beauty regimen each

day, remember to start on the inside. Let God lavish the luster of his Spirit on you, and see what a difference it makes.

Take a look at Proverbs 31:30: "Charm is deceptive, and beauty is fleeting; but a woman who fears the LORD is to be praised."

Your inner beauty will never fade. Shine on!

SCRIPTURE

Matthew 6:28–30 talks about how glorious the flowers are. Read through that passage and remind yourself why you don't need to worry about beauty or anything else. God is taking care of you.

TALK WITH GOD

Lord, when I compare myself to some of my friends, I imagine that I don't measure up, because they are all beautiful. They have the best clothes and the cutest hairstyles. Help me to see them and to see myself as you see us. Help me to be all I can be for you. Amen.

WOOF

OKAY, LET'S DEAL WITH IT. No matter how perfectly you were created, you probably don't like something about yourself. That's just human nature. You might have the best hair or the nicest smile or the most wonderful cheekbones, but all you see is the flaw, the one thing about yourself that you don't like. In fact, you're pretty sure you resemble a canine.

When you worry about your looks — and who doesn't? — you forget a couple of things that are important. One is that you're much more than the person you see in the mirror. The other is that how well you get along in the world has more to do with what's inside your heart and mind than what's on the outside. A mirror can do no more than reflect an image. You, on the other hand, radiate natural beauty from within.

Some girls worry so much about their weight that no matter what size they are, they only see themselves as fat. Some girls have one small blemish and imagine that it sticks out like a sore thumb. But think about it: Do you choose your friends based on whether they're the right weight or height or have perfect noses? Or do you choose them because of who they are? When it comes to the important things, what you look like matters less than you think.

God chose you exactly as you are, and he sees you as perfectly amazing. That's a guarantee!

SCRIPTURE

You were bought at a price. Therefore honor God with your bodies.

1 Corinthians 6:20

TALK WITH GOD

Lord, thank you for making me as I am to be a blessing to you and to others. You know I don't always like myself or how I look. There's always something about me that annoys me. Help me to get over myself and see that what I really need to focus on are my attitude and my spirit. Transform me so that I reflect more of your image every day. Amen.

ban the
BULLIES

BULLYING ISN'T ONLY MEAN, it's a way one person tries to intimidate or frighten another person. Whether it's a third grader taunting a first grader on the playground, a teenager mocking or verbally abusing another teen, or Goliath taunting the Israelites, it's all the same bad vibe. It's a vibe God truly hates.

The prophet Isaiah spoke for God when he said, "I will put an end to the arrogance of the haughty and will humble the pride of the ruthless" (Isaiah 13:11).

Unfortunately, our culture is full of bullies. You see them hanging around school grounds, jeering at sporting events, or backbiting in the political arena. These days you even have to guard against Internet bullies who hide behind a computer screen and still try to intimidate you. And sometimes people you thought were friends become the worst bullies of all.

Recognize bullies for what they are, and then do your best to protect yourself and others from them. Never put yourself in any danger, though. While you can watch out for bullies, report them, and not respond to their threats, it's not your job to figure out why they're mean or why they bully others. It is your job, however, to pray for those people, asking God to deal with them in his way. It's also your job to let an adult know if you discover a child or another person being bullied. It takes courage, but you have that.

SCRIPTURE

There are six things the LORD hates,
seven that are detestable to him:
haughty eyes,
a lying tongue,
hands that shed innocent blood,
a heart that devises wicked schemes,
feet that are quick to rush into evil,
a false witness who pours out lies
and a person who stirs up conflict
in the community.

Proverbs 6:16–19

TALK WITH GOD

Lord, in today's world it seems like bullying is everywhere. I've heard about the things they do and read stories of teens who have been bullied so much, they took their own lives. I don't understand why people are so mean. Please protect me and my friends from bullies. Amen.

unwrapping
THE ONION

THE WAY YOU ACT, the way you speak, the way you follow your heart — all of these are indicators of the kind of character you're developing.

Character is unwrapped layer by layer, like the skin on an onion or a gift in fancy wrapping paper. What's inside is really what counts. What's inside shapes what's outside. If you follow the teachings of the Bible and love Jesus, you're God's girl from the inside out, and your character tells him and everyone else what's important to you.

It takes time to develop good character. So once you've got it, protect it. A thousand tiny choices have shaped your character, but it can be damaged by one foolish act. And sometimes what is outside can affect the inside. First Corinthians 15:33 reminds us that our character is shaped by the company we keep. That makes the friends you choose very important. While you can be friends with someone you don't agree with all the time, it's usually best to hang out with people who share your values. Without a healthy environment, your inner self can shrivel like a bad onion.

In fact, your friends are probably a lot like you; they're figuring out what they really value and what they don't. So at this point in your life, a lot of other people also influence your choices, like parents, teachers, and youth workers. You know you're in good company when the people around you look for ways to help you grow and discover what's important to you.

SCRIPTURE

Do not be misled: "Bad company corrupts good character."

1 Corinthians 15:33

TALK WITH GOD

Dear Lord, I know that I'm growing and learning and changing. I want so much for you to be proud of the person I am today. Strengthen my character in any way you see fit. Thank you. Amen.

the stars SHINE; they don't whine!

PHILIPPIANS 2:14 IS A GREAT ATTITUDE-ADJUSTMENT reminder. Whining may not be your thing, but you might have friends who have a way of making anything and everything seem like a dramatic screenplay. Sometimes we simply have to accept things and leave them in God's hands.

You can usually accept your friends as they are, whether they whine or not, but it might be harder to accept someone who is different from you, or who comes from another culture, or who holds a belief you don't understand. Perhaps you complain when you feel forced to deal with difficult things, or you whine that people from another culture should be more like you so it would be easier to get along. In those situations, you have to practice tolerance and gentleness, and perhaps even forgiveness. In short, you have to practice acceptance.

Imagine doing "everything without grumbling or arguing." That's a challenge and a goal to work toward, a way of shining your light brightly and effectively in a world where things aren't always easy. You have star quality when you give others room to be who they are, or even when you give yourself room to be who you are. God sees you and loves you and accepts you.

Shine your light and bring a little joy to someone else today.

SCRIPTURE

Do everything without grumbling or arguing, so that you may become blameless and pure, "children of God without fault in a warped and crooked generation." Then you will shine among them like stars in the sky as you hold firmly to the word of life.

Philippians 2:14–16

TALK WITH GOD

Lord, I know I don't always see myself or others in the best light. Sometimes I complain about things at home or at school. Help me to remember that my light shines brighter when I keep my focus on you. Amen.

anger ... just a letter short of DANGER

IF YOU LOOK AT CLASSIC LITERATURE, you may discover a guy named Aristotle. He was a renowned philosopher, and he had some interesting things to say about anger.

According to Aristotle, "Anybody can become angry—that is easy; but to be angry with the right person, and to the right degree, and at the right time, and for the right purpose, and in the right way—that is not within everybody's power and is not easy."

Basically, Aristotle was saying that although it's normal to get angry, it's not so easy to figure out if you're angry for the right reasons.

James 1:19–20 puts it this way: "Everyone should be quick to listen, slow to speak and slow to become angry, because human anger does not produce the righteousness that God desires."

So what should you do when you lose your cool? The first thing you can do is pray. Ask God to help you listen and keep calm so you can have the life God wants for you. Then look at Aristotle's words and decide whether you're actually angry with the right person, to the right degree, for the right reason, in the right way, at the right time. If not, change gears. No matter how angry you feel, you can do it.

Take a walk, exercise, get some fresh air, and get your head clear. Pray and remind yourself that human beings aren't perfect, and even good friends can mess things up. You can turn anger around if you're quick to listen and slow to speak. Remembering to do so will serve you well.

SCRIPTURE

Take a look at the example in John 2:15–16 when Jesus was angry with the money changers in the temple. Anger does have a place.

TALK WITH GOD

Lord, I get bent out of shape more easily than I like to admit. Sometimes people push my buttons, and I don't like it. Please help me listen with my heart before I let my mouth spew out words I might regret. Amen.

making good CHOICES *isn't easy*

IF YOU WATCH REALITY-TV SHOWS, you've probably been surprised at some of the choices people make. In front of millions of viewers, they choose potential life partners, lose weight, become singers and dancers, or find out how smart they are. All those shows are about decisions or choices. But if it takes an audience to make a good decision, how do the rest of us manage on our own?

Your life may not have the drama of a weekly TV show, but it certainly offers countless opportunities for making decisions. Every day you make important choices, but your decisions can change from day to day for various reasons, or because of conflicting emotions. Take homework that a teacher assigns on Friday, for example. Sometimes you might rush home and do it right away just to get it out of your hair. Sometimes you might make a study date with a friend for Saturday afternoon so you have good reason to put it off. Now and then, you might rush through your homework late Sunday night while listening to your iPod, knowing you didn't really give it your best.

You make similar choices all the time, and each time you probably get a very different result. As a teenager, your life is swirling with choices, and it's tough to be clear about how to make the right ones. However, God has one command for you: "Choose ... this day whom you will serve" (Joshua 24:15). In other words, are you going to choose God or not? See how Joshua asked Israel to make this choice in Joshua 24.

Anytime you have to make a choice, try to be as informed as possible about your decisions, and then consider what God might have you do. God's a whole lot better than a viewing audience, and his guidance can make an eternal difference.

SCRIPTURE

Take a look at I Kings 18:21, where Elijah the prophet tells the people that they need to choose between worshiping God and worshiping Baal.

TALK WITH GOD

Lord, it sure isn't easy to make good choices sometimes. Please help me listen for your voice whether I'm choosing what to watch on TV or when to do my homework or which friends to hang out with. I want to be a wise and faithful girl. Amen.

stepping out of your COMFORT zone

LIFE IS COMING AT YOU FAST! You've got tryouts for the school play, a huge history term paper due way too soon, and a best friend who's mad at you about something you haven't even figured out yet. It makes you uptight and uncomfortable, like wearing a pair of stilettos with pointy toes.

Look at the story from Mark 4, when Jesus and his disciples were in great need of a little peace and quiet. They got into a boat and headed across the Sea of Galilee. They'd had enough of the crowds, and they simply wanted a little time-out.

What happened, though? They got into the boat, and suddenly the winds came up and the waves pummeled them mercilessly. The disciples thought they would capsize and drown. While they got more and more uptight about the storm, Jesus was propped up on a pillow, taking a little nap.

How could he sleep through a storm? What was he doing just dozing away when their lives were in jeopardy?

When you're feeling a little shaky about all you have going on, or when you're out of your comfort zone, you can choose to get dramatic and imagine the worst like the disciples did. Or you can kick off those pointy shoes and choose to believe that your loving God has your life so much in his hand that he wouldn't let anything happen to you without a reason. You can be comfortable when you trust God to watch out for you.

SCRIPTURE

I lie down and sleep;
I wake again, because the LORD
sustains me.

Psalm 3:5

TALK WITH GOD

Lord, some days I get rattled. I get a little crazy when I have too many things going on at once. Walk with me today and help me to trust that you know all the details about me and have me safely in your hand. Amen.

WHATEVER!

IMAGINE THAT YOU'VE NEVER HAD ANY PASSION for anything. You've never loved pizza or your dog or your best friend. You've never loved the color red or the fact that the stars look like millions of diamonds in the sky. You just don't care ... about anything. It's all just so-so. Whatever.

Now imagine that when Jesus came to earth, he was wishy-washy about his ministry. What if he had said to his disciples, "Go ahead, follow me if you want, but if you don't, no worries. It doesn't matter. Do whatever you want." Would anyone have followed him? Would there even have been a reason for the cross?

Your passions and the things you really love are what lead you to make a commitment. You're not lukewarm. You're definite about what you think. You're either hot or cold, and that's a good thing.

Revelation 3:16 is emphatic about God's desire for you to make a full commitment. He doesn't want wishy-washy, on-again, off-again followers. He wants commitment. He wants passion.

You might love pizza hot out of the oven or cold from the fridge, but the room-temperature pizza that sat out on the counter all day may not have much appeal. Your commitment to God and the things you believe requires you to draw a line in the sand and stand on one side or the other. Where do you stand?

SCRIPTURE

Because you are lukewarm—neither hot nor cold—I am about to spit you out of my mouth.   Revelation 3:16

TALK WITH GOD

Lord, I know I don't always keep my commitments. I don't want to go to church some Sundays or read my Bible every day. Help me see how much those things mean to you and to our relationship. Help me honor my commitment to you. Amen.

sticks and STONES

YOU MAY NOT THINK you have compassion built into your DNA, but you probably have moments when you feel empathy or special consideration for others. It may be when you see a tiny baby at church or a puppy with a hurt paw. It may come out when a friend is having a bad day or your little sister just needs someone to pay attention to her, and you know you have a little time to spare. However it shows up, your compassion pleases God.

Jesus's death for our sins was the ultimate act of compassion. He wanted so much for us to have a life with his heavenly Father that he was willing to do whatever it took to make it happen.

When the woman described in John 8 was caught sinning, a lot of people wanted to come and throw stones at her. They believed they had a right to judge her and get rid of her because she did something wrong. But what did Jesus say to those ready to hurl rocks?

He asked them one question: Have you ever sinned?

Not one stone hit the air.

Compassion means you care about others because you recognize that people are human and that everyone is part of God's story. Whenever you're not sure about how to show compassion for someone else, think about the compassion God has already shown you.

SCRIPTURE
Read the story in John 8:1 – 11 about the woman caught in adultery, and remind yourself to stop and think about God's compassion before you judge others.

TALK WITH GOD
Lord, I can jump to conclusions. I think I know what's going on when someone does something that offends me. But maybe I don't. Maybe I need to remind myself that I'm not perfect either. Please help me to be more compassionate and never to throw stones at someone else. Thank you. Amen.

being the best you POSSIBLE

SOME GIRLS JUST EXUDE CONFIDENCE. They walk into the room and everyone looks up. They're popular, and everyone wants to be included in their party.

Other girls are quieter, even shy. They rarely speak up in a gathering of friends and find it hard to let others in. They often hang back and step away from the popular crowd.

Whether you're more like the first group of girls or the second one, you need confidence to be the best you can be. Confidence is a bit like courage; it has to come from the One who can back you up on a moment's notice. For example, if you believe in what you're talking about, you're usually more confident to speak. If you've done your homework, researched the facts, and put everything together in your own mind, it's easier to confidently share what you know.

In Acts 4 we read about a special kind of confidence the Holy Spirit gave new believers. This confidence helped them speak boldly about their faith in Jesus. They believed God wanted them to get the news out, to be his voice and his hands and feet.

If you want to have more confidence speaking up in a group, it helps if you've done your homework, and it helps to check in with your faith in God. When you read your Bible and pray, your confidence grows. Why? Because you're in a relationship with a living Father who is always there for you.

Talk to him, and he'll strengthen your walk and your talk. Be the girl you want to be, and do it with confidence.

SCRIPTURE

For the Spirit God gave us does not make us timid, but gives us power, love and self-discipline.   2 Timothy 1:7

TALK WITH GOD

Lord, I'm building my confidence and my faith in you. Help me to keep stepping closer to you so that I can gently lead others to you and so that I can be myself in any situation. Amen.

where's the PEACE?

THE THEOLOGIAN MARTIN LUTHER made this comment on conflict: "Think of all the squabbles Adam and Eve must have had in the course of their nine hundred years. Eve would say, 'You ate the apple,' and Adam would retort, 'You gave it to me!'"

Conflicts are normal, and they arise in big ways and small ways all the time. Some conflicts are with and around other people—your parents, perhaps, or even good friends. You may not always agree with those who share your life.

Other kinds of conflict arise when you try to do too many things at once. Something usually suffers. If your homework doesn't get done because you need to practice the piano, you may get a bad grade. If you don't practice the piano because you have too much homework, you won't play as well. It can be tricky to schedule activities without running into conflicts.

Conflicts also happen in the area of your values or the ways you choose to live your life. Friends may decide that it's okay to go to a movie your parents already advised you not to see. You have to choose whether to listen to your parents' advice or blow it off and go with your friends anyway. If you blow it off, you'll find yourself in conflict with your heart, because you know you chose to ignore your own values.

The main goal, then, is to have peace of mind in everything you do. When you're at peace, you'll like yourself better, have more to give, and be more in control of the daily dramas that come your way.

SCRIPTURE

Therefore, since we have been justified through faith, we have peace with God through our Lord Jesus Christ, through whom we have gained access by faith into this grace in which we now stand.

Romans 5:1–2

TALK WITH GOD

Lord, I admit I'm not always at peace. I can churn things up at home or at school without even realizing I did it. Please help me get right with you in all my choices so that I can be at peace in all I do. Amen.

lions and tigers and bears ... OH, MY!

YOU ARE COURAGEOUS! That's right, even when you're facing scary things. Now and then, though, life hands you some unexpected curves, and, well, you can't be brave about everything ... right?

Perhaps, but the truth is that you have someone better than the the Wizard of Oz to help you stay on course; you have Jesus. He holds you up and keeps you close. He strengthens your steps.

What takes a lot of courage for you? Is it talking to a boy you like or singing in front of a group or sharing your faith? Maybe all those things cause you to pause and regroup or muster some bravado.

Walt Disney once said, "All our dreams can come true, if we have the courage to pursue them."

It takes courage to face a new day, to strive to do better, to work to become something more than you are at this very moment, to laugh at yourself when you fall down. It takes the courage of your convictions and your heart.

You were born to do great things, and God wants you

to have the courage to be all you're meant to be. You're not a fictional character like Dorothy from *The Wizard of Oz*. You're a real girl with real challenges to face that will test your courage. The good news is, you're not alone. God is with you!

SCRIPTURE

The LORD is my strength and my shield; my heart trusts in him, and he helps me.

Psalm 28:7

TALK WITH GOD

Lord, there are certainly times when I need more courage to do the things that have to get done. I ask you to please watch over me, walk with me, and give me the courage I need every step of the way. Amen.

everybody's A CRITIC!

CRITICS ARE EVERYWHERE. They tell you what to think about new movies and new books. They analyze a sports team that trades a key player. They check to see how you dress and wear your hair. They tell you what to think and what to believe and who to call a friend.

So what good are the critics? They remind you that you're not invisible. Sometimes they motivate you to try harder or to be better at something. At other times, they press so hard that they cause you to throw in the towel. Then they've gone too far.

Unless you're an Olympic athlete, you probably don't like being judged. Yet most of us find it easy to judge or point a finger, cast a catty remark, or simply turn up the volume to let another girl know we've found her unworthy. We love that sort of thing ... as long as it isn't happening to us.

We think it's okay to give criticism, but we don't want to get any. In our minds, it's never justified. Matthew 7:3–5 puts this into the right perspective for us. Jesus said, "Why do you look at the speck of sawdust in your brother's eye and pay no attention to the plank in your own eye?" (vs. 3).

Wow! There's a good question. What does it say about us if all we need is a little grain of truth—a speck of sawdust—to get our tongues wagging about someone else, and yet we fail to see that we've got the whole board, maybe the whole tree, in our own eyes? It says back off and ease up on others!

SCRIPTURE

Do not judge, and you will not be judged. Do not condemn, and you will not be condemned. Forgive, and you will be forgiven.

Luke 6:37

TALK WITH GOD

Lord, I know I sometimes run off at the mouth about other people, especially when I'm mad at them for some reason. I also jump to conclusions about other girls just because of the way they talk or the way they dress. Help me to stop that. I know it doesn't please you. Amen.

what should I THINK about when I date?

THE WORD *DATING* may be a somewhat old-fashioned idea. Maybe you're really just "hanging out" with someone. If you're friends with a guy and you go to a movie as buds, is that a date? If you hang out with a guy and meet some friends for pizza, is that a date? If you text a guy all the time, is that dating? When does friendship turn into "dating"?

First of all, keep in mind that it's totally cool if you're not even interested in dating at this point. You've got a full load already with school, youth group, and other stuff, and dating just may not be on your radar right now. That's all good.

If you are dating, though, or you want to date someone on a regular basis, what's your take on how to do it right? What does God expect from you when you date? Here are some things to think about:

- You are God's girl first.
- You own your body, your heart, and your mind.
- You know how to make good choices.
- You can stay true to yourself and your values.
- You should have fun when you're dating.

Remember this wise advice from Proverbs 4:23: "Above all else, guard your *heart*, for everything you do flows from it" (emphasis added). Sometimes you'll be out with a group of guys and girlfriends, and you're just having fun. Sometimes you want a special one-to-one relationship with a guy—you want a date. It's great to date as long as you know who you are: You're God's girl first!

SCRIPTURE

The goal of this command is love, which comes from a pure heart and a good conscience and a sincere faith.

I Timothy 1:5

TALK WITH GOD

Lord, I really want a date or a boyfriend, but sometimes it gets complicated. Please help me to be willing to come to you when I feel unsure of things. Thanks for loving me so much. Amen.

is there a little EEYORE in you?

"Good morning, Pooh Bear," said Eeyore gloomily. "If it is a good morning," he said. "Which I doubt," said he.

"Why, what's the matter?"

"Nothing, Pooh Bear, nothing. We can't all, and some of us don't. That's all there is to it."

"Can't all what?" said Pooh, rubbing his nose.

"Gaiety. Song-and-dance. Here we go round the mulberry bush."

EEYORE HAS A DEFINITE VIEW OF LIFE, and it isn't usually optimistic. He sees things the way anyone might who has his tail attached with a thumbtack.

You might feel a bit like Eeyore sometimes, wondering what to do next or simply not caring what comes next. When that happens, or when the warning signs of depression rear their heads, it's time to take some action. Feelings of depression happen to everybody, but when you can't shake them off or when talking to your best friend doesn't chase them away, you need to give yourself permission to get a little help. It's not only okay, it's the right thing to do.

So who can help? Well, your family, your best friends, your church, your pastor, your school ... they all can help. Or you can get professional guidance from a counselor or have a physical to make sure you're not suffering from some kind of chemical imbalance.

The truth is that depression is painful, and like any other kind of pain, the best way to deal with it is to get to the bottom of it. Root it out before it takes a stronger hold. Just remember that God is with you too and will work things out for your good. He wants you to be a little more like Winnie-the-Pooh and see the bright side of life. Eeyore probably just needs a nap.

SCRIPTURE

And we know that in all things God works for the good of those who love him, who have been called according to his purpose.

Romans 8:28

TALK WITH GOD

Lord, I'm not really sure what's going on with me. Please help me to get back to the joy you want me to have, because I know I can't do it on my own. I need your help to lift my spirits. Amen.

GOD'S fan club

DEVOTION IS A GREAT WORD. It means you're "all in," and you're not holding anything back. It means you're a big fan—a stick of dynamite couldn't shake your direction or get you to change your mind.

Jesus's followers were part of his fan club. They watched him, protected him, followed him everywhere, and believed in him. They were devoted to him.

You've probably indicated that you're a fan of someone on Facebook ... a rocker, perhaps, or an actor. Fans offer their adoration and love without hesitation, even without conditions. When their favorite person hits the tabloids in a negative way, they simply don't believe the story.

Well, what about your story with God? If you're a fan of God, maybe you need to show your devotion a little more. When the news tries to convince you that faith in God is a crazy notion, you need to don your favorite "I love Jesus" T-shirt and step up to the plate. God wants his fans to speak up, and that means you.

Oh, sure, he can get the work done with or without you,

because nothing will stop his story from unfolding, but he wants to show his glory through *you*, through *your* love and devotion.

Go on. Tell him how you feel. Show him a little devotion today.

SCRIPTURE
Follow the way of love and eagerly desire gifts of the Spirit.

1 Corinthians 14:1

TALK WITH GOD
Lord, I'm one of your biggest fans. I know I don't always show it, but I love you with my whole heart. Thanks for being there for me every day. Amen.

making friends with good CHOICES

IF DISCERNMENT HAS A BFF, IT'S WISDOM. These two go together like Batman and Robin, and they do everything they can to support each other. They are the dynamic duo of good choices. Sure, you can choose not to be discerning, and you can choose to close your eyes and walk into doors, but that will probably sting a little.

Think about the choices you made recently. Did any of them require a little extra thought? Did they beg you to think more clearly and to be wise before you acted? Maybe you don't have to be discerning when you're deciding what kind of pizza you like. But it may be a different matter if you're choosing whether or not to go to a party that won't be chaperoned. You're always choosing something.

The writer of Proverbs has some advice about making choices:

> Do not let wisdom and understanding out of your sight,
> > preserve sound judgment and discretion;
> they will be life for you,
> > an ornament to grace your neck. (3:21 – 22)

Well, you may not be thinking that discernment is chic jewelry, but it certainly could be a lifesaver. After all, making a good choice can mean the difference between tears and laughter, joy and regret, and a host of other things.

Make friends with discernment. It may be one of the best pals you'll have in life. Oh, take wisdom along too.

SCRIPTURE
Consider carefully what you do.

2 Chronicles 19:6

TALK WITH GOD
Lord, I know I need to think twice about things before I act. Please guide me and help me to remember that I need to slow down sometimes to make good choices. Amen.

how do you know what's RIGHT?

IF YOU ASK TWENTY DIFFERENT PEOPLE how to determine what's right and what's wrong, you'll probably get twenty different answers. How do you know what's right?

You may have friends or family who say that you have to decide. You have to figure out what's right for you. There's some truth in that. You do have to discover the right path—the one God intended for you. So how do you do that?

Here's one place a girl who wants to honor God in her life can start: prayer. Yep! That's the first step, because you need to check in with God and ask him to help you understand what is right. What's right sometimes depends on a situation, and it isn't always posted in large, black-and-white print. Sometimes there are a number of right possibilities. Your job is to ask God to help you understand the situation and choose what he wants for you—what is truly right.

After that, look at yourself in the mirror and imagine how you might feel if you make one choice over another. You can't always depend on what you feel, but your feelings can help to guide you, so it's worthwhile to consider how a given choice might make you feel down the road.

Talk with your parents. Believe it or not, they have to make choices all the time too. They have to figure out what's right for them. Find out what they do when they aren't so sure of their choices.

Ask your pastor or youth leader. Once you get the skinny from a number of reliable sources (okay, you might even add some of your friends here), you'll have a much better chance of making wise decisions and right choices.

In your heart of hearts, you'll have a sense of peace whenever you make an effort to do the right thing.

SCRIPTURE

Do not forget to do good and to share with others, for with such sacrifices is God pleased.

Hebrews 13:16

TALK WITH GOD

Lord, I really want to do the right thing. I don't always know what that is, though. Please help me to check in with you and those who know me best when I have a hard choice to make. Amen.

doubt and faith—
TWO SIDES
of a coin

PART OF YOUR FAITH EXPERIENCE and your life experience is about figuring out what's true and what you can believe. It's about knowing when you can trust your eyes and ears and senses.

Imagine how excited Peter must have been when Jesus invited him to step out of the boat and walk toward him on the water. He was probably honored to be called out of the group, excited as he watched Jesus easily navigating the surface of the deep, and pumped when he got out of the boat and found he could actually stand. Whew! Awesome!

But then something happened. Though Peter got out of the boat in perfect faith, sure that he could meet Jesus, before long his natural mind took over. His head started considering the impossibility of walking on water. His heart rushed with amazement, and somewhere in there, doubt slipped into his consciousness.

Suddenly doubt changed things. Water walking seemed too hard to imagine, and with each thought, each worry, Peter started sinking.

Hey, girl ... what about you? How quick would you have

been to get out of the boat? Maybe you would have started out confidently, but with the first twinge of doubt about your actions, you would have clammed up and sunk, just like Peter.

We call Thomas the doubter because he had to ask Jesus for proof before he believed in his resurrection. We give Peter grief over not being able to walk on water. But if you had been in their sandals, would you have been able to put your faith first, or act on faith without needing more proof?

Never doubt that God loves you and watches over your steps every minute.

SCRIPTURE

Matthew 14:22–31 will remind you not only of what happened to Peter, but what can happen if you let fear lead the way instead of faith.

TALK WITH GOD

Lord, I know I don't always have the faith you'd like me to have. I ask you to be with me and encourage me through those moments when I lose ground and start sinking into doubt and fear. Help me not to doubt anything about you. Amen.

what TIME IS IT?

THE WRITER OF ECCLESIASTES got it right when he said there is a time for everything. There's a time to take action, a time to express feelings, and a time to help others. What time is it for you?

If you're like most girls, you're often driven by your emotions. Your hormones are raging, and you can feel silly one minute, way too serious the next, and downright weepy after that. Who knew you could feel so many different things in one day? Oh, God knew! He made you just the way you are!

If you read any of the Psalms, you'll see that David did his fair share of crying in front of God. He soaked his pillow more than once in an effort to get his feelings back on track as he cried out to God to help him through his fears and sorrows.

If you buy into the premise that God loves you, then you have to know that he understands you're an emotional being. He designed you so that you could express everything from laughter to tenderness to three-hanky crying spells. You're his daughter, and he thinks it's quite okay for you to have a good cry now and then.

Your emotions may spin around like a twisted roller coaster. You can expect them to keep changing and take you places you haven't gone before. But God will protect your emotions and keep you gently and lovingly in his care. There's "a time to weep and a time to laugh," as it says in Ecclesiastes 3:4, and there's a time when either of those emotions is exactly the right thing to do.

SCRIPTURE

Take a look at Psalm 6:6–7. See how David freely shared his emotions with his Father, God.

TALK WITH GOD

Lord, I'm glad you see me just as I am, happy and with it one minute, and weepy and all undone the next. I thank you that I can be myself with you, no matter what's going on in my life. Amen.

a case of the "CAN'TS"

IT ALL STARTS WITH SOME FOGGY NOTION that you can't do something ... anything. You can't get the part you want in the school play; you can't go to camp this year; you can't get the guy you like to like you back—the list goes on and on. It's downright discouraging, and the more you think about things, the bigger the list gets. Whew! It's amazing you've gotten this far!

Fortunately you have friends, family, and other people in your life who notice your struggles when you're in the land of the "can'ts," and they hold up enough light so that you can start to see your way clear to actually move forward again. They do a good job, but you have another cheerleader in your corner too. You have God on your side, and you and God are a majority against anything.

In Paul's second letter to the Thessalonians, he offered this wonderful wish: "May our Lord Jesus Christ himself and God our Father, who loved us and by his grace gave us eternal encouragement and good hope, encourage your hearts and strengthen you in every good deed and word" (2:16–17).

Well, write that one on a Post-it and stick it on your mirror. God gives you "eternal encouragement and good hope." If you've got that kind of encouragement, you might just have to get over your case of the "can'ts," because all God wants from you is the "cans." See what he can do though you today.

SCRIPTURE

Whatever you have in mind, go ahead and do it, for the LORD is with you.

2 Samuel 7:3

TALK WITH GOD

Lord, I know I get discouraged pretty easily, and then I start thinking I can't do anything, or at least I can't do anything right. Please help me see what I can do. Give me a case of the "cans." Amen.

let's be ENEMIES!

SOMETIMES YOU GET A LITTLE TIRED of walking on eggshells around one of your friends. You know the one—she pushes you a little too often; she says things behind your back and then "apologizes" and acts like it's no big deal, without really fixing the situation. She simply doesn't seem to get how to be a good friend.

One solution might be for you to decide it's okay for the two of you to start from scratch and be enemies for a little while. Sometimes when you have an enemy, with a little time and skill, you can make that person into a friend.

If you can't reconcile with people you put on your enemy list, what can you do for them? Jesus has an answer. He says to pray for them—oh, and love them. Pray for the bad guys? Love the people who make you miserable? Well, yes.

Did you know that you once were God's enemy? It's true. Before you confessed your faith in Jesus, God had to keep you outside of his family circle. He had to draw a line around you and wait for you to get to another place in your thinking. He did that because he wanted to be able to call you his friend. Jesus said that he can call any of us friends once we share our belief in him.

It's always a good day to turn an enemy into a friend. If you can't do that just yet, then pray for those who bug you and love the ones who don't seem very lovable. When you do, you may just change the course of their lives.

"Let's be enemies" may turn into "Let's be friends."

SCRIPTURE

Take a look at Matthew 5:43–48.

TALK WITH GOD

Lord, I try not to even think about the people I don't like or who don't like me. It's going to take some doing, but help me want to pray for them. Help me want to love them. Thanks for loving me. Amen.

we all FALLDOWN sometimes

WOW, YOU BLEW THAT ONE! It's going to take some real effort to get back on track. Sure, you're disappointed. But guess what? You may have failed to deliver this time around, and you may not have come out on top, but things happen, and you can't always win. So get up and try again.

The opposite of success isn't failure. It's giving up and not making an effort. But you can try again. What you may need is just a little reminder of the tools you have in your toolbox, the things that will help you win the day next time.

The first tool is your mirror. That's right! Go look in the mirror and ask the girl you see what she really wanted. Did you want to win? Did you want the lead in the school play? If you think about why you might not have achieved your goal, it could have something to do with you. You might not have prepared well enough, or you might not have wanted the success. Sometimes success simply means working longer and harder all the time. That might not seem like much fun.

The next tool is to have a conversation with your mom and dad. Share your disappointment and tell them how you feel. Find out how they feel and what they might have done differently. Find out about an experience they may have had when things didn't work out as they had hoped.

Finally, talk to God. Tell him everything about your experience. Ask him for wisdom in figuring out what to do next. Share your heart and give him a chance to help you.

We all fall down sometimes. The trick is learning from that tumble and getting up again as quickly as possible.

SCRIPTURE

As long as [King Uzziah] sought the LORD, God gave him success.

2 Chronicles 26:5

TALK WITH GOD

Lord, I try and try, and sometimes no matter what, I don't seem to get where I want to go. Please help me to keep trying and to believe that you know what's best for me. Help me to talk with you before I try anything important. Amen.

FAITH *is a verb*

MARTIN LUTHER SAID, "Faith is a living, busy, active, powerful thing; it is impossible for it not to do us good continually."

What a great definition! It's a reminder that faith isn't just about philosophy. In fact, it's not even a question of debate. It's something you do, more than just something you talk about. So how do you have an active, living, busy faith?

Maybe another question is, how don't you? Imagine a day coming up next week. You already have plans, maybe a unit test in history, a sleepover at a friend's house, and a babysitting job. Those are just the planned things, and along with them are the chores you have to do at home, your homework, your responsibilities at church and in youth group. Imagine all that, but without the element of faith. How does that feel?

Now give God the go-ahead to walk through your plans and help you see what might work well and what might not. Give God the chance to lead. When you do that, you won't even need a flashlight to get to the next steps. You'll know that your steps are assured.

Living out your faith is exciting, constant, and sometimes difficult. When you have trials to go through, your faith gets bigger. When you share your heartfelt gratitude, it expands.

Keep the faith, girl, because it will keep you all your life.

SCRIPTURE

Without faith it is impossible to please God, because anyone who comes to him must believe that he exists and that he rewards those who earnestly seek him.

Hebrews 11:6

TALK WITH GOD

Lord, I really do want to be full of faith every day. I want to trust you, walk with you, and believe in you. I want to, but I don't always do it well. Please help me live my faith today. Amen.

this crazy FAMILY

TOLSTOY SAID, "All happy families are alike; each unhappy family is unhappy in its own way."

Is your family a little bit crazy? You know, maybe your dad teases your mother about her hair in front of friends, and your mother rolls her eyes. Maybe your brother ran away at fifteen and lives with your cousin in South Dakota. Maybe you live with a single parent, or you live with your grandparents.

The thing is, in whatever form it presents itself, the place you call home is the place where you live with your family. They may be fabulous, and you might feel really blessed, especially as you think of some of the stories your friends have shared about their families. Or your family may be unpredictable, leaving you slightly on edge all the time, or they might just not be the people you picture when you imagine a great family.

A little craziness is actually pretty normal in most families. At best, a family is meant to provide a place where you can grow and learn and become the best possible you. If you're blessed with a family of believers, you'll grow in the love and knowledge of the Lord.

There will be days when you may just wonder how you got into your family. What's a nice girl like you doing with people like that?

The answer is you're a nice girl learning and growing and becoming a woman cherished by God.

SCRIPTURE

God sets the lonely in families.

Psalm 68:6

TALK WITH GOD

Lord, I don't always understand my family. They're a little quirky. I guess you knew what you were doing when you put me here, though, so help me to be someone who makes my family proud. Amen.

run, hide, embrace FEAR!

SOMEONE COINED THE ACRONYM **FEAR,** which stands for "False Evidence Appearing Real." Wow! That's pretty cool when you think about it.

So what is false evidence? If you see a shadow cross your path as you walk home on a moonlit night, is it a signal of danger? Possibly, but it could also just be a shadow cast by a cat at a curtained window. Within seconds, though, fear grips you and you don't really care what it is, as long as you get home safely.

You may see a big spider on the floor and wonder how you're going to get past it. It's definitely real. There's no denying that, but you're hundreds of times bigger than the spider and a whole lot scarier, so which of you should really be afraid?

Fear could be the opposite of love. It's what stops you from moving forward, prevents you from thinking wisely, promotes your insecurity.

One writer said that a coward gets scared and quits; a winner gets scared and keeps going. You can break the power fear has over you simply by moving on. You can face it squarely, look at it directly, and starve it to death. If you don't feed your fear, it can't survive. And one way to starve the fear is to turn to God, praying about what scares us.

Make a little list of the things you're afraid of and pray about them. How many of them can you do something about so that you can cross them off the list forever? If you listed something you need help with, chat with your parents or your pastor or youth counselor. Let those who love you help you grow.

SCRIPTURE

There is no fear in love. But perfect love drives out fear, because fear has to do with punishment. The one who fears is not made perfect in love.

I John 4:18

TALK WITH GOD

Lord, I am kind of skittish sometimes. I know that you protect me and love me. Please help me to get over the somewhat silly things I feel afraid of so I can move on and share more of the joy I have in you. Amen.

the
RIGHT FIT
for you

IT'S NORMAL TO WANT TO FIT IN with the girls you hang with most. It feels good to be like them in the way you dress or the way you think and talk. That's why it's so important to be careful when you choose new friends. After all, what they say and do will influence you. That's what makes you great buds.

Fitting in is fine to a point, but you also have to know what's right for you, what makes sense for the girl you really are. Have you ever seen photos in fashion magazines where they show one celebrity wearing a beautiful dress, and it looks great on her, but when they show another celebrity wearing the same dress, it just doesn't do it for her? It's not the right fit or style for her body type.

To some degree, the same thing can happen in your friendships or in the choices your friends make. A particular choice can be okay for them, even work for them, but that same thing may not work for you. For example, you may have a friend who wears really tall, strappy heels, and she looks great in them, and they never seem to bother her feet. But if you tried to wear those heels, they'd kill you in the first twenty minutes. They just aren't your style.

God wants you to be the real you and be careful about your choices. He doesn't want you to conform to the thinking of your friends. He wants you to be the unique work of art he created you to be. So as you consider the friends you want to hang with, the choices you want to make, and the things you want to have influence you every day, remember to be yourself. After all, you are a Designer creation, and there's no one quite like you.

SCRIPTURE

Blessed is the one
   who does not walk in step with the
    wicked
or stand in the way that sinners take
   or sit in the company of mockers,
but whose delight is in the law of the
LORD.

Psalm 1:1–2

TALK WITH GOD

Lord, thanks for making me uniquely me. Help me to remember that it's all right for me to look to you for guidance, because you know everything that fits me best. Amen.

let's say WE'RE SORRY ... but you go first!

WHEN YOUR FRIEND DOES SOMETHING that really yanks your chain, you might be tempted to just walk away. After all, you don't need the aggravation, and you've got other friends, so just forget about it. Yep! Sometimes that's the way to go ... sometimes, but not very often.

So what other choice is there? *You* can say "I'm sorry." Wait a minute! You aren't the one who did the damage. It wasn't you who caused the problem; she did! *She* needs to say "I'm sorry."

Sometimes forgiveness means you should go first. Remember that God did exactly this for you. Jesus wanted you to have a way to be forgiven when you make mistakes, and even though he didn't make any, he gave his life knowing you'd be coming along and someday need a chance to tell God you're sorry. God sees you in a different way then and says that your sins have been cast far away and he doesn't remember them. Why? Because you have Jesus standing in the gap, linking your heart to the heart of God.

So think about it. Is it more important to prove who was right? Or is it more important to offer the white rose of forgiveness? It's more fun to have your friend back, and with a little forgiveness tossed in, you'll both grow in your relationship.

Life will bring you lots of good chances both to forgive others and to be forgiven by others. You'll always get to choose who's going to repair the relationship first. Just keep in mind that everybody needs a little forgiveness sometimes.

SCRIPTURE

"I will put my law in their minds
   and write it on their hearts.
I will be their God,
   and they will be my people.
No longer will they teach their neighbor,
   or say to one another, 'Know the LORD,'
because they will all know me,
   from the least of them to the greatest,"
declares the LORD.
"For I will forgive their wickedness
and will remember their sins no more."

Jeremiah 31:33–34

TALK WITH GOD

Lord, I know that I make mistakes and mess things up sometimes. Help me to remember that when someone does something that annoys me. Help me to be a forgiving person. Amen.

A FRIEND
like you

YOU PROBABLY HAVE A GOOD FRIEND OR TWO. You may have been friends since grade school, or you may have just met recently. Whichever way it is, a friend needs your time, your support, and your silly jokes. You need each other, but what does it really mean to call someone a friend?

On one hand, a really good friend is the one you can be yourself with. That means you can try on that short striped skirt with the crazy T-shirt, and she'll be willing to tell you it just isn't you. You can talk about life over pizza, share your ups and downs over ice cream, and just be together doing nothing at all. You're friends, pure and simple.

Henry Ford noted, "My best friend is the one who brings out the best in me." That's important for you too. You want to spend time with people who not only get who you are but help you become even more, who cause you to stretch sometimes, bend sometimes, and relax sometimes. Friends do that for each other.

When you follow Jesus, you become God's friend. You begin a relationship with him, and only you can decide how deep it will go. Are you going to keep God at a distance and treat him like an acquaintance, or are you going to visit with him on a regular basis, get to know him, and allow him to be in your best-friend circle?

You'll win friends and lose friends, but what's most important is figuring out what kind of friend you are. Ralph Waldo Emerson said, "The only way to have a friend is to be one."

Go on. Be a good friend to others, and you'll always have big reasons to smile. In fact, everyone will want to have a friend like you.

SCRIPTURE

One who has unreliable friends soon comes to ruin,
but there is a friend who sticks closer than a brother.   Proverbs 18:24

TALK WITH GOD

Lord, help me to be a good friend to other girls and guys in my life. But more than that, help me to be a good friend to you. Amen.

give a little, GET A LOT!

OKAY, SO LET'S TALK ABOUT GIVING. What makes it better than getting?

The world tells you all the time that you deserve to get good things. You deserve the best clothes, the best guy, the best grades, the best shoes ... you name it. You may not know why you deserve them, but it's probably because you're really special. Well, on one level it's true. You are really special ... after all, you're God's girl, the daughter of the King.

On the other hand, special is as special does. In other words, you become more special and more deserving by your actions, your willingness to put others first, and your efforts to be a giver. The fact is, more blessings come from giving than from simply receiving. You may have noticed that truth already.

How and what can you give? One writer put it this way: "Give strength, give thought, give deeds, give wealth; give love, give tears, and give yourself." You give by being present, by being there for someone else. You offer the hand of friendship, a kindhearted thought, a little encouragement.

You put yourself out for someone else. That's how you become a giver, a generous friend.

Don't you love it when someone does great things for you? Hold that thought and give a little. In fact, become the most generous girl you know. If you do, it won't matter what you get back.

SCRIPTURE

In everything I did, I showed you that by this kind of hard work we must help the weak, remembering the words the Lord Jesus himself said: "It is more blessed to give than to receive."

Acts 20:35

TALK WITH GOD

Thank you, Jesus, for the people who are so generous to me. Help me to learn from them and be willing to be a great giver to those around me. Amen.

sticky
FINGERS

YOU'VE PROBABLY BEEN PART of some fund-raising efforts by now. Maybe your youth group needed money to take a mission trip or your high school class needed money for a field trip. Maybe you had a bake sale or sold magazines or T-shirts to get the job done. In the end, you got what you needed, and it was great.

What else did you get, though? First of all, you got together with other people who had a similar goal. You got real satisfaction in the work you did together, and you learned a thing or two about the way people give. Maybe you understood for the first time the difference between people who give you a few bucks begrudgingly, making you feel like you had to pry the money from their sticky fingers, and people who give from the heart. Those people not only gave to your cause but helped you get the word out and made sure you had a bigger network to pursue. They were the really generous ones with their money, their time, and their connections.

That's giving! It isn't just about money. It's about what

motivates you to be a giver. It's about the spirit of being a giver. In fact, it's about learning to be a giver God's way. God wants you to be someone who knows how to give—a girl who gives with her whole heart.

If you ever realize you're withholding something you know you could give, something God's Spirit is prompting you to give, then you need to take notice. After all, you don't want to be one of those people with sticky fingers.

SCRIPTURE

Proverbs 11:24 highlights two kinds of givers: "One person gives freely, yet gains even more; another withholds unduly, but comes to poverty."

TALK WITH GOD

Lord, help me be aware of the ways I choose to give to my friends and family. Teach me to follow your example. Amen.

"God bless you" IS NOTHING to sneeze at!

IT USED TO BE IMPORTANT FOR A GUY to ask a girl's father for his blessing before the guy could propose marriage to her. It was considered the proper thing to do to make sure the father was pleased with the man who wanted to take his daughter away from him.

This doesn't happen often anymore, but it may help to illustrate the point of why a blessing is important. Just like the nervous would-be groom who wants to impress the father and make sure to get his blessing, we want to know that God blesses the things we do too. We want our work, our lives, our days to be blessed by God.

In biblical times, a father's final blessing was essential to his children. The father actually bestowed upon his children the will and favor of God. That's why there was such a fuss over the moment when Isaac blessed his sons, Jacob and Esau. Jacob actually stole the blessing from Esau, taking his birthright, which was a serious, permanent thing. Read through the story sometime in Genesis 27.

Today, though, we talk about blessing someone as though

it were no more important than a sneeze. We say "God bless you" to any sneezer passing by. We may really mean those words, but the challenge is to extend God's blessings to everyone we meet.

When your Father in heaven blesses you, things happen. You are then blessed to be a blessing to others. Spread the sunshine. Giving and getting blessings is important. Bless someone else today.

SCRIPTURE

I will make you into a great nation,
and I will bless you;
I will make your name great,
and you will be a blessing.

Genesis 12:2

TALK WITH GOD

Lord, I thank you for blessing my life in so many ways. Help me to be a blessing to other girls in any way I can. Amen.

cut me
SOMESLACK!

SOMETIMES YOU JUST NEED A BREAK! You need everybody to step back and give you a little more room to figure things out yourself. You're overwhelmed and need space, but more than that, you need grace.

We all need a little grace. In fact, we need a *lot* of grace, and we need the kind God gives. His gift of grace does more than cut you some slack; it gives you room to grow and learn and make mistakes. It's a huge umbrella of free will, with the understanding that he'll watch over you and bring you safely back if you get too far away.

Living under God's grace is like getting fresh air. You walk in it and talk in it, and everything you do stems from it. Nothing can keep you from breathing in his air of grace, and nothing can separate you from the love of God, as Paul wrote in Romans 8. You didn't do anything to deserve God's grace; it's just one of the great benefits of being a believer.

Does the grace of God mean you can do whatever you want or don't worry about what God wants for you? Does it mean you're free and clear of every sin? No, it just means you can fall down and get up again. It means that your faith in Jesus opens new doors and windows for God to see you and watch over you.

That said, you may want to remember to cut other people some slack when they need it. Give them the grace of coming back to you when they've made a mistake or made a fool of themselves. We all do it. We all need grace. Thank God for his grace and pass it on to others!

SCRIPTURE

To each one of us grace has been given as Christ apportioned it.

Ephesians 4:7

TALK WITH GOD

Lord, I'm sure glad you're willing to give me room to make a few mistakes. I know I need your grace all the time. Help me to give others the same kind of room. Amen.

GOD
loves me?

SURE, YOU'VE BEEN SINGING "Jesus loves me, this I know" since you were just a little bitty girl, but do you really get it? Do you really know that because Jesus loves you, God loves you? Well, do you?

If you've ever gone through some bad stuff where you told yourself the story that God probably doesn't love you anymore, then you'll understand why we're talking about this. After all, there's not a girl out there who hasn't messed up now and then, and it's a bummer. It can be a landslide that gets you stirred up so badly you're not sure anyone loves you, much less God.

If you remember Romans 5:8, it says that God demonstrated his love for us. How? By giving us a way back to him through Jesus. In other words, God started the relationship. God initiated a chance to get to know you, guide you, and be part of your life. Why? Because of his love for you.

Charles Spurgeon said, "He who counts the stars, and calls them by their names, is in no danger of forgetting His own children. He knows your case as thoroughly as if you were the only creature He ever made, or the only saint He ever loved."

God knows your case. He knows you. He sees you all the time, and is always thinking about how wonderful it is to have you to love. All he wants from you is a relationship where you show him that you love him too. Like any good relationship, the more love you show, the more you'll feel, and the more you give, the more you'll get back.

God not only loves you, but he loves you big-time! He gave his only Son for you!

SCRIPTURE

Keep yourselves in God's love as you wait for the mercy of our Lord Jesus Christ to bring you to eternal life.

Jude v. 21

TALK WITH GOD

Dear God, I don't always understand why you love me. I'm not very lovable sometimes. Help me to be more of the kind of girl you want me to be. Amen.

hitting the
TARGET

AS YOU MOVE AHEAD in school year after year, you start to get a sense of what you're good at. You know that you're great at English but pretty lame at math, or you're great at volleyball but better off staying away from ballet. You keep learning about yourself, and with that information, you try to figure out what you're going to be someday. You start to imagine what kind of work you might like to do or where you might like to go to college. It's a great time to plan for the future.

The good news is that you're not making all your plans by yourself. God has a stake in what you do. In fact, he's working hard to guide you toward what he already knows is going to offer you the opportunity to do the work that will make you the happiest and be the most fulfilling. He knows what will not only satisfy your brain and your talents but will also satisfy your heart. How does he know? Because he made you!

Psalm 139:16 says,

Your eyes saw my unformed body;
all the days ordained for me were written in your book
before one of them came to be.

In other words, God knew you before you were even born. He made plans for you.

Now as you make plans to go on to college, or go on a mission trip, or take tap dance, know that God has you in his sights and has definite plans for you too.

SCRIPTURE

In their hearts humans plan their course, but the LORD establishes their steps.

Proverbs 16:9

TALK WITH GOD

Lord, I'm always making lists and starting new things. Help my plans to be in line with your plans so we both win. Thanks so much. Amen.

a taste of GOD'S SPIRIT

SPRINKLE A LITTLE SALT INTO YOUR PALM and take a look at it. Now toss it into your chicken noodle soup. Can you still see it? Probably not, but it's still there. If you need to remember it's still there, just taste a spoonful of soup and see for yourself. In some measure, that's a way to help you understand how God is there, how he is with you even when you can't see him.

If you think you can only find God when you go to church or when you're at a campground by an open fire singing praise songs, then you've missed something. You've missed knowing that God is with you all the time. It's helpful to think of God as being within you and without you (that is, outside of you), before you and behind you, beneath you and above you. Wherever you look, God is there. He is *omnipresent,* which means he's able to be everywhere at once.

When you get a little extra tug at your heart or a sense of warmth and peace permeates your whole body through prayer and meditation, you may really feel God's incredible presence.

In biblical days, those who encountered the Spirit of God spread themselves facedown on the ground at his feet. They knew that they were in the presence of holiness. God's holiness is so powerful that you cannot stand very close to it. You would fall down too.

Out of his love for you, though, God allows you to feel his presence in little doses. Of course, he's always there, but like the salt in your soup, you can't always tell. Once you get a taste of his presence, though, it makes you want another helping. God is with you today!

SCRIPTURE

Better is one day in your courts
than a thousand elsewhere;
I would rather be a doorkeeper in the
house of my God
than dwell in the tents of the wicked.

Psalm 84:10

TALK WITH GOD

Lord, thank you for being with me all the time, even when I can't feel you. Help me to be aware of you and to reach out to you every day. Amen.

hanging on to
EVERY WORD

DID YOU EVER MEET AN ACTOR OR A ROCK STAR? Chances are you found yourself wrapped up in everything they had to say, hanging on to every word. Celebrities say a lot of things. Sometimes they speak from the heart; other times they speak words someone else told them to say. Words have a lot of power, and it's important for you to be careful with them.

God wants you to hang on to his words too. Can you imagine the people in the crowds who had a chance to see Jesus and hear him speak? It must have been so awesome to hear him speak with such kindness and authority. It must have made their hearts tingle and their minds wonder who this person could really be.

That tingly feeling could happen to you. When you read in your Bible the words Jesus spoke, and you take them to heart, you're hanging on to his words. You're so in tune with what he had to say that those words are imprinted in your brain like a rock song. You can recall them anytime.

You may not have a lot of experience reading God's Word. If it's new to you, give yourself credit for getting started. Take time to get through the Gospels and see how the authors wrote about their experiences with Jesus.

The fact is, you can experience God's Word for yourself whenever you want to. Just open your Bible and ask the Holy Spirit to guide you as you read. Underline the verses that sing out to you. Say them out loud. Get involved with the Word. When you do, you'll be just like the groupies who follow a rock star. The big difference will be that Jesus is worthy and can really lead you into all that is good. Hang on to his every word!

SCRIPTURE

All Scripture is God-breathed and is useful for teaching, rebuking, correcting and training in righteousness, so that the servant of God may be thoroughly equipped for every good work.

2 Timothy 3:16 – 17

TALK WITH GOD

Lord, teach me, guide me, and lead me through your Word. I'm ready to be your groupie. Amen.

don't fan the
FLAMES

GOSSIPY GIRLS HAVE TROUBLE keeping everything straight. After a short time, they forget who they told what and how they may have embellished their tale. The thrill for them is in having the information, seeming important for a moment, and getting other people's attention. Once they muddy the waters, they move on, looking for other peaceful shores to disturb.

Watch out for the girls who always find another way to talk about you, even if they rarely talk with you. After all, discovering the truth isn't the game for them. Being a friend isn't the game either. Information is a form of power, and whether it's true information or not, it can be heady to share other people's bad luck or poor choices.

Sometimes gossip even shows up in a prayer group. Someone tells about a situation that they hope the group will address with prayer, only to have someone else take it outside the group. Be careful about spreading other people's news. It could come back to bite you.

So today don't fan the flames when someone tries to lure you in with some juicy gossip. Tell the gossiper that you have better things to do. Stand up for the person being talked about, and suggest that it might be better for everyone to know the whole truth before spreading rumors. You can make a big difference!

SCRIPTURE

Without wood a fire goes out; without a gossip a quarrel dies down.

Proverbs 26:20

TALK WITH GOD

Lord, I know I've shared things I shouldn't about someone else. Remind me that I don't need to add any fuel to the flames, especially when I don't know the truth about the info being shared. Help me to be a good friend, not a gossip. Amen.

a million THANKS!

IF YOU WROTE on two-inch square pieces of paper all the things in your life that you have to be thankful for and then put all the papers in a jar, how big a jar would you need? Just for the sake of a visual, let's say you'd need one the size of the space shuttle. That's probably not big enough, but it would be a good start.

Don't believe it? Just for fun, take five categories and write as many thanks as you can under each one. For instance, you might choose My Health, My Family, My Church, My Talents, and My Lifestyle. See how many reasons to be grateful come to mind. Oh, and don't forget to be grateful for your mind, because it's giving you the chance to think, which gives you the chance to learn and try again. You get the idea.

Here's another example. Matthew Henry, the great Bible scholar, made these comments when someone took his wallet: "Let me be thankful first, because he never robbed me before; second, because although he took my purse, he didn't take my life; third, because although he took all I possessed, it was not much; and fourth, because it was I who was robbed, not I who robbed."

It's great to see Henry's thinking about this incident. He found all the good things about the robbery and was truly grateful. When something happens to you that makes you cringe a little, follow his example and see if you can find any good in the experience.

You may not come up with a million reasons for gratitude, but if you kept a record over time, you may be surprised at how many things happen to you for which you can be truly grateful.

SCRIPTURE

Thanks be to God! He gives us the victory through our Lord Jesus Christ.

1 Corinthians 15:57

TALK WITH GOD

Dear Lord, I'm really happy about all the things you've done for me. Thank you for my friends and my family and for giving me everything I need to live today. And thank you for Jesus, though I know I can never thank you enough. Amen.

get into your right-sized CLOTHES

DID YOU PLAY DRESS-UP when you were a little girl? Perhaps you had fun pretending to be your mom or a pretty princess going to the ball. Or maybe you liked to pretend that you were the teacher, and your class had to do all the work you assigned them. There's something fascinating about being all grown up, unless you're the one doing the growing!

You're in a huge personal growth spurt. You're growing in every area of your life. Sometimes it feels great, but at other times you might wish you could just be a little girl again. Growing up is complicated.

Some girls try to hurry to become a grown-up. They wear clothes that aren't very appropriate for girls their age, or they go too fast in a relationship with a boy and end up with a child or with great shame and guilt. The fact is, God designed you to grow up gradually. The *Jack and the Beanstalk* story doesn't fit you. Nothing grows through the roof overnight.

The Bible talks about gradual growth. It speaks of growth in grace, growth in knowledge, growth in faith, growth in love, growth in holiness, growth in humility, growth in spirit, and in other areas too. God wants you to learn a little bit at a time about what it means to be you. You're growing so much, you might not recognize yourself three months from now.

So go ahead and grow! Grow in love toward God. Grow in kindness and in giving. Grow in ways that will make your family proud. That's what God wants of you. Keep trying on different clothes, but wear the ones that are just right for you.

SCRIPTURE

Like newborn babies, crave pure spiritual milk, so that by it you may grow up in your salvation, now that you have tasted that the Lord is good.

1 Peter 2:2–3

TALK WITH GOD

Lord, I think I'm growing up okay. Sometimes I like pretending I'm an adult. Other times, I like it when I can cuddle up in my daddy's arms and be a little girl. Thanks for being the kind of Father who watches me grow with love. Amen.

a little help for
MY FRIENDS

THE BEATLES HAD A LOT OF HIT SINGLES. One of them was a song that suggested a person could get by with a little help from his friends. The truth is, we all get by that way sometimes. Friends do a lot to keep you feeling okay about yourself and about life in general.

But let's look at this idea in a different way. How about being the one who helps your friends, being the reason your friends can get by?

God wants you to help others and be compassionate. Jesus often told his disciples that it was important for them to take care of the poor. Of course, in those days there were no social systems in place for people to be activists and givers. United Way and the like didn't exist. People had to depend on one another whenever they needed help.

So how can you help others? Are there girls and guys you go to school with that nobody else pays attention to? Maybe God wants you to expand your friendship circle. Next time you go into the lunchroom, look around. Is someone sitting all by themselves, pretending to read books or count the ceiling tiles? Maybe they need a new friend. What about at your youth group or on your girls' basketball team? There are lonely people, hurting people, and people just in need of a little friendship everywhere you turn.

If you really want to serve God, then take care of his flock. His people are everywhere.

SCRIPTURE

[God says,] "If you lend money to one of my people among you who is needy, do not treat it like a business deal; charge no interest. If you take your neighbor's cloak as a pledge, return it by sunset, because that cloak is the only covering your neighbor has. What else can they sleep in? When they cry out to me, I will hear, for I am compassionate."

Exodus 22:25–27

TALK WITH GOD

Lord, I'm sure there are girls in my school that I haven't paid any attention to. Help me see them as you see them, and move my heart to do what I can to be a friend. Amen.

little
WHITE LIES

WHEN YOUR MOM ASKS YOU where you've been and you respond, "At Susan's house," only you were at the mall with Susan and some friends, is that a lie? Oh, it's okay because your mom isn't wild about you hanging out at the mall, so a little white lie should take care of things.

But imagine that your mom is at the grocery store, and your neighbor stops her for a chat in aisle 10. "Oh," your neighbor says sweetly, "your daughter is growing up so nicely. I just ran into her over at the mall on Tuesday."

Little white lies can lead to big, swamp-monster lies, the kind that get slimier the further you go with them. Sure, you can rationalize that everyone lies sometimes, but that still doesn't make it right. What causes you to want to lie, anyway?

If you don't like the family rules, like not going to the mall on a weeknight, then talking about it and getting some more input from your parents might help. After all, they probably have a good reason for a "no malls on weeknights" rule. Take a look at what happened to a married couple named Ananias and Sapphira in Acts 5. They lied to Peter, but he declared that they had actually lied to God, and they suffered the consequences.

Yikes! Could little white lies be considered lying to God? Take some time today and make sure you're telling the real story, no matter who you talk to or what you say.

SCRIPTURE
The LORD detests lying lips, but he delights in people who are trustworthy.

Proverbs 12:22

TALK WITH GOD
Lord, forgive me for telling those little white lies I sometimes make. Help me to be a girl of great integrity. Amen.

does hope have FEATHERS?

EMILY DICKINSON WROTE,

> Hope is the thing with feathers
> That perches in the soul,
> And sings the tune without the words,
> And never stops at all.

Hope keeps you humming even when you don't know the words. It reminds you that the music is playing in the background, and if you keep listening, you'll be able to hear it. Before you know it, you'll be able to sing along too.

Most of us would be in deep trouble without hope. Hope provides you with a goal, something to look forward to. Remember when you wanted a princess doll for Christmas almost more than anything else, or maybe a pair of ice skates? Weeks before Christmas, you thought about how wonderful it would be to have tea parties in your own private castle with your doll, or how it would feel to twirl around on the ice in your new skates. You began to hope for the thing you wanted most and waited for it with as much patience as you could muster.

Nothing has changed. You still need to hope for the things that you believe will make a difference in your life, even if it's not Christmas. Traditional hope means that you're not quite sure it's available to you, but that you believe it could happen anyway. Christian hope implies that you understand God can do anything—eagerly anticipating something will happen because he promised it would.

Perhaps hope does have feathers, because our minds seem to fly from one hope to another. Even so, the best hope we have is in Jesus. Put all your hopes and dreams in his hands, and he will guide you to their fulfillment.

SCRIPTURE

May the God of hope fill you with all joy and peace as you trust in him, so that you may overflow with hope by the power of the Holy Spirit.

Romans 15:13

TALK WITH GOD

Lord, I know I sometimes hope for silly things, so fill me with hope for the things you really want for me. Let me hope for the good that comes from you. Amen.

is my FACE RED?

DID YOU EVER DO SOMETHING that embarrassed you so much you got all red-faced and could hardly speak? Maybe you drank some soda and let out a big burp in front of the cutest boy in the school. Well, relax! Everyone has been there. It doesn't feel good, but it does do one good thing: it makes you a bit more humble.

Humility brings a little checks-and-balances system into that troublemaker called the ego. Humility reminds you that you're not perfect and that everyone (including you) makes mistakes. Doing something embarrassing may give you a red face, but contrary to how it feels, you won't die!

Being humble before God lets him know that you recognize your limitations. You realize that you are only the clay, and he is indeed the Potter. If he formed you, if he created you for a particular purpose (and he did), then it's really uncool for you to put yourself on a pedestal. You didn't create anything that he didn't allow you to create.

Today, as you go about your schoolwork, practice for the gymnastics meet, or catch some downtime with your friends, remember that everything you have and all you are exist because of one thing: God loved you so much he gave you the world. Take a little time to say a humble thank-you today.

SCRIPTURE

For those who exalt themselves will be humbled, and those who humble themselves will be exalted.   *Matthew 23:12*

TALK WITH GOD

Lord, I hate it when I do something stupid and embarrass myself in front of my friends. But I hate it even more when I go around acting like I'm all that. Help me let go of my pride and give thanks and praise where it really belongs—to you. Amen.

I'M ME, and you're not!

WHEN YOU GO SHOPPING with your best friend, and she buys cool dangling earrings, do you feel slightly pressured to buy some too? Maybe she's taller than you are, so earrings like that are pretty flattering. You, on the other hand, got the short gene, so those long earrings would be sitting on your shoulders. But this is about friendship, and real friends like doing a lot of things the same way. Right?

It's cool to do things the same way your friends do them, but it's also cool to step aside, stand apart, and be absolutely wonderful you. You can create your own look, have your own great personality, and actually, you may find it all makes you so unique that more people are drawn to you just for being you.

Who are you? You're the girl God created for a very special purpose. He's grooming you, watching you grow with great pride, and helping to mold you into the young woman he wants you to be. When God sees you, he goes right past your hairstyle, your new jeans, and whether or not you're slightly over- or underweight, and looks at one thing: your heart. He wants your heart always to be something he can keep shaping. He wants to speak to you there, guide you there, and give you his love right there.

You may want to be just like your friends, but God wants you to be just who you are. He wants you to say, "I'm me, and you're not." Being you is what makes him smile, because you're his girl.

Show him your best self today.

SCRIPTURE

I praise you because I am fearfully and wonderfully made.   *Psalm 139:14*

TALK WITH GOD

Lord, I like being me. Help me always to be the person you planned for me to be, even when I'm around my best friends. Amen.

get a GRIP!

YOU'RE SMART. YOU GET IT. You know when someone is putting you on or when they are giving you a story straight up. Well, God does too. He knows when you come to him half-heartedly, and he knows when you come with your heart in your hand. He prefers the real, honest, authentic you above all else. He wants you to get a grip on what it means to be a young woman of integrity.

You can't turn integrity on and off with a button. You either operate that way or you don't. If you do, bravo! If you don't, why don't you? Test yourself a little. What do you do when you get in a tight spot? Say you're a person who usually gets her homework done, but one morning as you head into math class, you remember that the teacher had given an extra assignment, and you were supposed to log on to find it on her digital Blackboard. You totally spaced it. Now you're going into class with no time to do the work.

It turns out you're on her radar this morning, and she asks you to solve the first problem on the website. What do you do? Oh, and to make matters slightly more complex, your good friend Josh sees the dilemma and pushes his paper close to you so you can read from it. What's your choice?

When your value system says that you must operate with integrity, your conscience will be your guide. Integrity is like honesty on steroids. It's a big part of who you are, and it says a lot about you.

Today, do everything with integrity. Get a grip on what's real and right for you.

SCRIPTURE

For you were once darkness, but now you are light in the Lord. Live as children of light (for the fruit of the light consists in all goodness, righteousness and truth) and find out what pleases the Lord.   *Ephesians 5:8–10*

TALK WITH GOD

Lord, I try to do the right thing most of the time. It's tricky, though, when I get backed into a corner. Please help me to always be honest with myself and others. Amen.

what you KNOW for sure

IF YOU'VE EVER LOOKED through Oprah's *O* magazine, you may have noticed that she has a monthly column titled "What I Know for Sure." In that column, she usually shares something she has learned or observed about the world and the personal truths she has drawn from her observations. Whether or not you buy into her conclusions and make them your own is up to you. The thing that's good about it, though, is that she has taken a stand and has decided what her view of something really is.

You're smart. You're also a girl who has to make a lot of choices. Sometimes you may be a bit foolish in what you choose, and other times you'll be brilliant. When it comes to things of God, though, you need to realize that what the world thinks is smart may not be so to God. What the world thinks is foolish may delight God to no end.

As it says in 1 Corinthians 3:18 – 21,

> Do not deceive yourselves. If any of you think you are wise by the standards of this age, you should become "fools" so that you may become wise. For the wisdom of this world

is foolishness in God's sight. As it is written: "He catches the wise in their craftiness"; and again, "The Lord knows that the thoughts of the wise are futile." So then, no more boasting about human leaders!

God's definition of wisdom isn't the same as the way your friends, or even Oprah, might define it. Anytime you really want to know for sure, go to God, and he'll help you understand everything with perfect clarity.

Perhaps what you know for sure is that you don't know what you don't know, but God has you in his grip today and always.

SCRIPTURE

The beginning of wisdom is this: Get wisdom.
Though it cost all you have, get understanding. Proverbs 4:7

TALK WITH GOD

Please help me, Lord, to be smart enough to come to you with anything I don't understand. Give me wisdom every day. Thank you. Amen.

the lousy part of JEALOUSY

LET'S SAY YOU ARRIVE LATE to your friend's birthday party. When you get there, you discover the guy you've had your eye on for some time is really being flirty with a girl you don't care for very much. The last time you connected with this guy, it seemed to you that the two of you had a chance of starting a great relationship, and you came to the party hoping to connect further. Now you're really upset, and the party isn't much fun. That's the lousy part of jealousy!

Step back a moment, though, and look at what happened. All those emotions, stories playing in your head, are just that. They're in your head. You have no idea what the guy thinks of the girl he's talking with or what he thinks of you. It may turn out that when he sees you, he'll finish his conversation and wander over to you. It may turn out that he's happy where he is. Either way, your feelings of jealousy won't change a thing except to give you a headache and cause you to have one bummer of a time at the party.

There's a reason why jealousy is often referred to as the green-eyed monster. It rears its ugly head and makes everybody in the room uncomfortable. It jumps to conclusions, often the wrong ones. God wants you to have good judgment and to recognize when someone is treating you unfairly. He also wants you to know the truth about any situation. Seek first to understand the other person before you try so hard to be understood. Jealousy will never serve you well.

SCRIPTURE

When [Joseph's] brothers saw that their father loved him more than any of them, they hated him and could not speak a kind word to him.   *Genesis 37:4*

TALK WITH GOD

Lord, I know I jump to conclusions sometimes just because jealousy gets the best of me. Help me to find out the truth before I take action or form opinions. Amen.

fudging
JUDGING

SOMETIMES YOU MAKE EXCELLENT CALLS. You know when to draw the line, and you do. At other times your judgment isn't as good. You try to fudge a little on what you know is right. You think maybe you can bend the rules a bit. But could you bend so much you break?

You're always judging something. You might judge how much time it will take to do your homework or how long you'll be visiting with friends. You might also judge some other girl's outfit or her hairstyle. You might even judge that you like it and tell her so, or that you don't like it and therefore don't like her either. It's not the best use of your judgment, but it's easy enough to rationalize. After all, everybody does it. Of course, that kind of thinking never proved the majority was right.

Sometimes you judge yourself even more harshly than you judge others. You may be too hard on yourself about the way you look or how much you weigh. You may judge your family as not being as cool as someone else's family. The trouble is that you're often not seeing the whole picture, or maybe you're just focusing on the wrong part.

God wants you to wake up! He wants you to be very careful anytime you judge things, especially when you judge yourself or others. After all, the only one really fit to judge human beings is God. He set the standard, and it's his judgment call that we all hope has mercy attached.

Remember when you go to make any kind of judgment that it's best to do it with wisdom and mercy. Ask God to keep you close to him anytime you have to make a judgment call.

SCRIPTURE

Stop judging by mere appearances, but instead judge correctly.

John 7:24

TALK WITH GOD

Lord, I'm guilty of judging others without really thinking about what I'm doing. Help me to be aware of that, and help me to be kinder and more loving to everyone around me. Amen.

DESIGNED
to be kind

THE WORLD DOESN'T NEED any more nasty people! After all, you can pick up the daily paper in any city in the country and read horror stories about ways that people can be mean to one another. What can you do to help balance things out, to keep from being one of the nasties and be one of the niceys, if there is such a word?

Every Christmas, it's fun to think of the Santa Claus that Clement Moore created, looking to see who the good girls and boys might be. The nasty ones aren't going to get any presents. Sometimes we wish God took that stand, not giving his good gifts to nasty people, but he doesn't seem to work that way. On second thought, that's probably good for us, since we have days when we might not be nice enough to get anything either.

You were made to be kind to everyone, though. You know it because God gave you a big heart to sense when others are in need or in pain. He gave you the gift of compassion to help others out when they're struggling. If you see a girl at school who is having a hard time learning a new computer program, help her. That's being kind. That's using the big heart God gave you.

There's a popular saying, "If you were arrested for being kind, would there be enough evidence to convict you?" Look for opportunities to offer a kind word, a helpful hand, a little tutoring to others. You'll see people everywhere who need your good side, maybe even the people in your own family. Plant evidence of your kindness everywhere.

John MacDonald said, "If I can put one rosy sunset into the life of anyone, I shall feel that I have worked with God." Well, you were designed with everything you need to paint some rosy sunsets in the lives of people around you. It's the kindest thing you can do.

SCRIPTURE

Anxiety weighs down the heart, but a kind word cheers it up.

Proverbs 12:25

TALK WITH GOD

Lord, help me remember that everyone out there is struggling a little. Let me be an example of all that it means to be kind. Amen.

what's your
PLATFORM?

IF YOU'VE EVER RUN FOR STUDENT GOVERNMENT, you've probably had to do a little campaigning. Some girls are natural-born leaders, and it's easy for them to stand up in front of people and give passionate speeches. Others aren't as fond of public speaking, so it's more of an effort to get up in front of the whole class or the whole school and say a few words.

Leaders have to have a platform—a vision or some particular goals they're trying to achieve. They then have to get others to follow or support their goals in order to get things done. You're a leader anytime you set things in motion to guide others.

If you're the chairperson for the prom committee, you're leading the group. If you're a counselor at summer camp, you're a leader. If you think your own thoughts and cast your own vision for the goals you've set—where you want to go to college or what career path you'll take—you're also a leader.

In every case, though, you have a platform. Jesus was a leader, and his platform was the fact he's the only way back to his Father, there for all the people who would choose to believe in him. He wanted to change the way people lived and the way they treated each other. Some would even call him a rebel.

Leadership isn't always about being in the limelight to get things done. Sometimes leaders are humble people who work tirelessly behind the scenes and also manage to change the world. Mahatma Gandhi was a leader, and so was Mother Teresa. They caused things to happen, and you can too.

The more you connect with God, the more you understand who you are and your mission as a daughter of the King, the more you'll take your place and build a platform of his love.

SCRIPTURE

By day the LORD went ahead of [the Israelites] in a pillar of cloud to guide them on their way and by night in a pillar of fire to give them light, so that they could travel by day or night.

Exodus 13:21

TALK WITH GOD

Lord, please lead the way for me as you have for your people in the past. I want to build a platform of love and joy that helps me lead others to you. Amen.

THAT'S LIFE
... deal with it!

HAVE YOU EVER NOTICED how easily we resign ourselves to the things that drag us into the pits and blow them off with a wave of the hand? "That's life," we say. "What are you gonna do?"

In that statement, we give away all the power God gave us. We act as if we're puppets on strings, without any choices. The truth is, God cut those strings already, and we're free to make life choices any hour of the day. In other words, you aren't expected to resign yourself to the pitfalls; you're expected to rise into the joy he meant for you to have. Having an abundant life is partly about what God does and partly about what you do.

As Charlie Brown said, "In the book of life, the answers aren't in the back." In other words, it's up to us to seek God's guidance for the answers because he gave us the book. He just wants us to read it so that every time a test comes, we'll be ready to pass it with flying colors.

Some people go around trying to figure out the meaning of life. Others walk around half-asleep, not really getting into the story of life at all. God wants you to deal with life in a way that says you understand it's a journey, a sacred trust between him and you, and that you both strive to make it wonderful.

Today, and with every breath you take, you have the choice of embracing the life you have and making it everything you can or of simply waking and sleeping, waking and sleeping; humming but never singing; missing all that God has for you. It's your choice and your day. What will you do with it?

SCRIPTURE

I have come that they may have life, and have it to the full.   John 10:10

TALK WITH GOD

Lord, help me to be happy with what I have but eager to explore all that you want for me each day. Help me to live my life fully. Amen.

walls or BRIDGES

A WRITER NAMED JOSEPH FORT NEWTON said that "People are lonely because they build walls instead of bridges." When you want to make friends but you have your walls up so high they couldn't even pole vault over them, or you're so busy hiding out that they can't find you, you end up with no friends. It's ugly. It makes you feel alone in the world.

You may be able to tell yourself the story that it's other girls who make it hard for you to have friends, but how many bridges have you attempted to build to get across to them?

One of the first things God noted after he made Adam and placed him in the garden was that Adam was lonely. He wandered around naming the animals, adjusting to his new home, and yet he felt aimless. God saw that and decided it wasn't a good thing, so he made Adam a mate. He gave Adam a friend and a life partner so that he wouldn't be alone. Okay, so Adam and Eve were made for each other, but you have to make your own friends. So what will you do?

If you're struggling with shyness or doubts about who

you are, or you don't feel worthy of friendship, then ask your youth pastor or someone else you trust for some ideas. Take little steps to get where you want to go. You don't have to change yourself or the world overnight, you just have to work toward the goal of being able to build a bridge to friendship. You have to be willing to let down your guard and get rid of a few walls.

It's a new day, and you're a wonderful girl. Take a peek out there and ask God to help you find a genuine friend.

SCRIPTURE

The LORD God said, "It is not good for the man to be alone. I will make a helper suitable for him." Genesis 2:18

TALK WITH GOD

Lord, you know it's not always easy for me to make good friends. Help me let my guard down a little and find the kind of friend you would choose for me. Amen.

LOVE STUFF

LOVE IS ONE TRICKY BUSINESS. It seems like everywhere you turn, the word shows up, but with a different meaning. You know, there's the love you have for rich, gooey chocolate sauce on your favorite ice cream, the love you have for your parents, and the love you have for God. Then there are the cute red shoes you just love that you saw at the store, and that sweet puppy up the street.

Hmm ... How do you figure out what love is about if you use the same word for all these things? Certainly the TV and magazine ads don't help. They seem to define love as seducing someone into liking you better, or they suggest that if you just had perfect hair or used the right breath mint, you'd be loved in a nanosecond.

It's safe to say you'll be defining what love really means to you most of your life. By now you have enough experience to know that there are lots of ways to love. When you think about what God wants for you, though, look at what Jesus defined as the greatest commandments: to love God with your whole heart and mind and soul and to love your neighbor as yourself. There you go—two ways to understand what love is.

If you love God with your whole heart, you'll think of him first, asking his direction in everything you do. You'll long to talk with him and spend time in his Word, because when you love someone, you want to be with them. If you then love your neighbors or the kids you go to school with as you love yourself, you'll figure out how to love others in good ways. You were made to love and to be loved, and though the world would offer you a thousand definitions, God has only these two. Let God guide you in matters of love.

SCRIPTURE

"Love the Lord your God with all your heart and with all your soul and with all your mind." This is the first and greatest commandment. And the second is like it: "Love your neighbor as yourself."

Matthew 22:37–39

TALK WITH GOD

Lord, help me to love from the bottom of my heart so that I stay true to you and true to myself in all that I do. Amen.

having
IT ALL

FOR MANY PEOPLE, life is about accumulating things. Teen magazines and the popular girls try to make you feel like you have to have it all. You may have friends who have huge closets full of great clothes or the best shoe collection you've ever seen. You may try hard to keep up with them, at least buying one pair of designer jeans so you fit in a little better, but it's just not your thing.

Madonna may have been a material girl when she was your age, but you're not. You're God's girl. You're clothed in his love and grace and goodness. As you grow in faith and understanding of what Jesus means to you, you'll see the world and your closet differently. You'll see the opportunity to go through your T-shirt collection and decide what you can donate to a shelter for teen girls who are less fortunate. You'll see a chance to volunteer your time to help someone struggling with math to do better.

Your faith gives you the opportunity to have it all. You can be full of treasures that won't fade away. You'll have more to give away with every kind word you share with someone who is hurting, and you'll discover a capacity for love you didn't even know was there. Your closet will be full of the things God wants you to have to do his work.

Don't get caught up in all the glittery ads. Don't buy into the idea that your clothes are just "oh so last season," because you're always current, always changing, and always being made new by God's love. Every day you're a new girl in Christ and a shining example of his love. Go on, have fun wearing a new T-shirt, but remember that the shirt isn't you, the shirt isn't the treasure. You're the treasure, and you are rich beyond measure.

SCRIPTURE

Do not conform to the pattern of this world, but be transformed by the renewing of your mind.   Romans 12:2

TALK WITH GOD

Lord, thank you for all the cool things I have. Thank you for loving me so much. Help me share all I have with those around me. Amen.

CHA-CHING!

IF YOU'VE EVER PLAYED MONOPOLY, you're familiar with how people can become really obsessed with money. After all, it's the object of the game to buy all the properties you can get your hands on and bankrupt everybody else. The one with the most property and toys wins.

Unfortunately, a lot of people play the game of life that way too. They look for ways to get more gadgets, more things, more money so that others will look up to them. It's their way of gaining power and respect. They can become obsessed with money.

Don't you find it fascinating that the King of the universe chose to live on this planet as a carpenter, doing a humble job? Isn't it interesting that he didn't try to gain people's respect by buying their friendship or offering them special treats? Yes, he fed them; in fact, he fed as many as five thousand of them at a time, but he wasn't materially wealthy. He was rich in the things that matter. He was totally connected to the One who owned Boardwalk and Park Place right from the beginning.

What is it about us that makes us want to have more and more and more? Yes, we need enough money to pay bills and pay our way in the world, but why do we need more than enough? If we have enough food, do we need to keep eating and filling our plates?

You need to be wise in the ways of money. If you're not careful, money will be your god, and you'll forget your purpose for being on earth. Let God guide you in matters of money, the way he does with everything else.

SCRIPTURE

Those who want to get rich fall into temptation and a trap and into many foolish and harmful desires that plunge people into ruin and destruction. For the love of money is a root of all kinds of evil. Some people, eager for money, have wandered from the faith and pierced themselves with many griefs.

1 Timothy 6:9–10

TALK WITH GOD

Lord, money seems like such a good thing, and sometimes I envy the people who have more of it than I do. Please help me to keep a healthy attitude about money all of my life. Amen.

having it YOUR WAY

IF YOU THINK ABOUT IT, you probably give an order to somebody nearly every day. It may be the order you give the woman at the pizza place, with very specific instructions about no red sauce or anchovies. It may be an order for a burger. No matter what it is, when you place an order, you want to have it your way.

In some measure, that's what God wants too. He made you, he loves you, and he's keeping you; and therefore, he has a job for you. It's part of your life purpose. He equips you to get the job done and then expects you to deliver.

Your parents also equip you and offer insights about life. They ask you to listen to them because they know the trouble you could get into if you shoplift or take part in underage drinking or something else you already know isn't right for you. They don't want you to get into trouble or get hurt.

God wants you to obey the rules, not because he wants to cramp your style, but so you have some guidelines and boundaries. If you don't have any limits, you don't know when or where you could get into trouble.

You may not think it's cool to have to be obedient to your parents or your teachers, or even to God. The fact is, though, that it's more than cool. It's what your Creator expects, the One who made you and knows you inside and out. He set the boundaries to keep you safe and well. Obeying him is your gift of deep respect and love for him.

SCRIPTURE

Do not merely listen to the word, and so deceive yourselves. Do what it says.

James 1:22

TALK WITH GOD

Father, I don't always listen to the rules you or my parents give me. When I go my own way, I think I'm being smart, but I end up feeling a little guilty. Please help me to listen to you with love and respect and obey what you ask me to do. Help me listen to and obey my parents too. Amen.

digging roots and finding WINGS

YOU'VE PROBABLY SEEN A QUOTE THAT SAYS, "There are just two things parents can give their children ... roots and wings." Your parents signed up for the job of giving you a great foundation and the opportunity to explore the world on your own when the time is right.

Your parents aren't perfect. You probably already know that. They certainly know that. The good news is that God didn't expect them to be perfect when he placed you in their care. He just expected them to pitch in, do as good a job as they can, and come back to him for parenting advice when they need it.

God knew they wouldn't get everything right or understand all your ups and downs, but he also knew they would love you and train you and help you make good choices. They love you even when you're cranky and just barely someone they can live with, as well as when you're practically an angel. God designed you in a special way, so he gave your parents patience, blinders, and grace to help you become what he wants you to be.

Grace is part of what makes any family work well, because each person has a personality that is unique. If you've tried babysitting for moody little kids, you probably have a good idea how difficult the parenting thing can be.

Your parents make sure you have what you need to succeed in school, to enjoy the good things about life, and to learn about God. Those are your roots. All too soon, your parents will step aside and give you one more thing with somewhat aching hearts. They will give you wings to fly from their nest.

Your parents are your soul support every inch of the way. Hang a little extra love on them today.

SCRIPTURE

When I was a child, I talked like a child, I thought like a child, I reasoned like a child. When I became a man, I put the ways of childhood behind me.

1 Corinthians 13:11

TALK WITH GOD

Lord, I know I don't always get the way my parents act or why they do the things they do, but I love them. Help me do the things that show I respect them always. Amen.

what's so good about WAITING?

YOU PROBABLY AREN'T REALLY THRILLED about waiting for things. Waiting to go to college, waiting to have a boyfriend, waiting to drive a car—it can seem like you've been waiting forever. The truth is, the real goals and achievements in your life are worth the wait. After all, once you get there, you'll set new goals and wait again.

It's good to get used to slowing your pace and taking a deep breath. Sometimes you have to wait for reasons that don't really matter to you. Maybe you have to wait for your sister to get back with the car before you can go do some window shopping yourself. Maybe you have to wait for your mom to finish her appointment with the accountant before she can take you out to dinner. Maybe you just have to wait in line at the grocery store.

Computer technology has trained us to think things happen instantly, but most of the time we have to wait a bit.

One writer said, "Patience is the queen of virtues." Practice that virtue, then, maybe with your scepter in hand, and wait for God to answer your prayers. F. W. Faber said, "We must wait for God, long, meekly, in the wind and wet, in the thunder and lightning, in the cold and the dark. Wait, and he will come. He never comes to those who do not wait."

Today, thank God for loving you even when you have to wait. Trust him to take care of you at just the right time, and get on with other things. The waiting will be worth it.

SCRIPTURE

You need to persevere so that when you have done the will of God, you will receive what he has promised.

Hebrews 10:36

TALK WITH GOD

Lord, thank you for all the good things in my life. You know the special things I'm still waiting for. Please wait with me and help me to be patient. Amen.

follow THE LEADER, not the crowd

AS A CHRISTIAN, you signed on to follow the One who makes a difference in your life today, tomorrow, and always. There's a place in your heart only he can fill, and like the disciples of old, you've given up things that might seem normal to others just to follow him.

If following Jesus makes a difference, then you aren't likely to be the same as everyone else in the crowd. Unfortunately, that doesn't mean you won't be tempted to do what all the other girls are doing. After all, it's not a problem for them, so why can't you join in?

Fair question! If it's about the latest cool jeans or whether to cut your hair in the style most other girls wear, then that's totally your call. Those are things you can choose, so rock on!

If you're talking about whether to start smoking because other girls in your circle do, but you know it's not really cool to you or your family, you may want to think twice. If you're thinking about getting a fake ID to get into a bar, hoping your parents won't find out, you're pushing the envelope.

Your choice to live in a way that pleases God isn't always

going to be easy. You may slip now and again and have to ask for forgiveness. You may make a foolish decision and have to live with the consequences. The key is, make sure your decisions are yours. If you decide to do something that is against your nature simply because your friends are doing it, the consequences may be tougher to deal with than you expect. You may find you followed the wrong crowd.

Jesus wants you to follow him, pure and simple. Pray for your friends when they make wacky choices, and pray for guidance so you can keep following your leader, Jesus, with great joy.

SCRIPTURE

Follow God's example, therefore, as dearly loved children. *Ephesians 5:1*

TALK WITH GOD

Lord, I don't always understand why I can't just do the things my friends are doing. Somehow, though, I know I'm different. Help me to keep following you every day. Amen.

lighting
YOUR FIRE

YOU ONLY GET TO BE A TEENAGER THIS ONE TIME, so grab your chance to explore your options. If you have a talent to sing or write music or strum a guitar, you may stand on a stage as a professional musician some day. If you have a talent for numbers, you may become an investment broker or a banker. All these things are built on gifts you have that you can develop if you choose. They're your potential.

Your potential for something develops in little ways. You start out putting on little skits for your family; they encourage you by laughing. You then cut up in school, and your classmates encourage you more, even when you're sitting in detention. Before you know it, you discover that acting is what you do well. Broadway may be calling one day.

The apostle James reminds us that a little thing like a spark can set a whole forest on fire. A spark of talent or interest can set you in motion for the fire God has put in you. Watch for those little things that draw your attention, the things you love to do, and the things that make your heart happy. Those things are the sparks of your future.

SCRIPTURE

The tongue is a small part of the body, but it makes great boasts. Consider what a great forest is set on fire by a small spark.

James 3:5

TALK WITH GOD

Lord, you know what's best for me. Guide me in big ways and little ways to discover more of what I can be. I know I want to be something great for you. Amen.

i'd pray if I JUST KNEW what to say!

DO YOU EVER THINK YOU SHOULD PRAY about something but then talk yourself out of it? Maybe you don't know what you want to ask for. Maybe you don't even know what the topic is. You just know that somehow you're not feeling very peaceful, and it's not about the moody side of PMS.

Instead of letting your hormones decide whether you'll pray, take another look at what the little voice in you is saying. Maybe redefine *PMS* as "Prayer Means Something!" In other words, prayer will get you the answers you're looking for, even when you don't know the questions.

Think of yourself as a kind of prayer warrior heading into a battle today, needing to be armed and protected. If you hold that image up, then spending a few moments in prayer will fortify you. Here's a helpful definition of a prayer warrior from Bill Hybels: "A prayer warrior is a person who is convinced that God is omnipotent — that God has the power to do anything, to change anyone, and to intervene in any circumstance. A person who truly believes this refuses to doubt God."

So it's not about having all the right words in your back pocket; it's about giving God a chance to help you with whatever is going on in your life. If you're happy, thank him! If you're confused, talk to him! If you're angry, shake your puny fist at him and see how he can help. Prayer is your chance to get things right again.

Pray! It may be the best chat you have all day.

SCRIPTURE

The Spirit helps us in our weakness. We do not know what we ought to pray for, but the Spirit himself intercedes for us through wordless groans. And he who searches our hearts knows the mind of the Spirit, because the Spirit intercedes for God's people in accordance with the will of God.   Romans 8:26–27

TALK WITH GOD

Lord, thanks for being there for me anytime, day or night. I'm not sure what I want to say, but I know you'll understand and help me figure it out too. Help me to hear your voice once more. Amen.

more proud, but LESS PRIDE

IT MIGHT SEEM CONFUSING at first to understand that you can indeed be proud of what you achieve, and proud of your hard work, as long as you build in a little modesty and humility. Where being proud of your A on the history test might get you in trouble is letting it turn into boasting. Boasting then turns into "see how great I am," not "see how great I did on this test," and that becomes pride.

Pride, as you probably already know, is the subtle tool the serpent used to seduce Eve into biting the forbidden fruit. He appealed to her ego and her pride. He even made her think she could be like God if she wanted to be. That was a temptation she couldn't resist. Her pride jumped in and wondered why she should listen to God when she could be just like God. Whew! That bites! That's a big one!

Sadly, there are those in history who have thought that they too might be gods. After all, they had command of huge armies, or they were the leaders of everything known to man. They had something no one else had, and what happened in every case? They fell because of their own arrogance. If you need some examples, take a look at Goliath, Samson, and King Saul. They all let pride bring down the house.

When you do well, God is proud of you. When you get an A or you perform well in sports or in the youth choir, everyone is pleased—and you can be too. The difference is between being proud of the moment, with a sense of thankfulness to God for giving you the talent to achieve in a special way, and going off on your own, thinking you did it all yourself. That's pride.

With God all things are possible. Without God, nothing is. (Because everything ultimately comes from God.) Give God the credit for making wonderful you just as you are.

SCRIPTURE

When pride comes, then comes disgrace,
but with humility comes wisdom.

Proverbs 11:2

TALK WITH GOD

Lord, thank you for all that I am, for sticking with me when I do well and even when I don't. If I feel proud, let me always give thanks to you for giving me what I need to excel. Amen.

first things FIRST!

YOU'RE PROBABLY USED TO KEEPING a schedule each day. You know that math class is at 8:45 and history is at 10:20. You know that on Tuesdays you have piano lessons from 4:00 to 5:00, and on Sundays you have youth group at 7:00. It's good to keep a schedule, but is that the same thing as knowing your priorities?

Setting a priority list helps you do the important things first. After that, it doesn't really matter what comes second. Sometimes you may get into a mess because you can't get all your homework done on time, or you can't get the big report for science finished by the due date. When that happens, it may mean you simply didn't give those things priority. When you don't take first things first, you sometimes don't get another chance.

C. S. Lewis, author of The Chronicles of Narnia, offers us this guidance about setting priorities:

The moment you wake up each morning, all your wishes and hopes for the day rush at you like wild animals. And the first job each morning consists in shoving it all back;

in listening to that other voice, taking that other point of view, letting that other, larger, stronger, quieter life come flowing in.

In other words, the best way to start your day is to quietly come before God in prayer and talk to him about all the stuff that's on your plate. When you make him the priority, he can help you be clear about what to do first. Give it a try and see if it helps you today.

SCRIPTURE

But seek first [God's] kingdom and his righteousness, and all these things will be given to you as well.   Matthew 6:33

TALK WITH GOD

Lord, please help me get things straight today. I know I'll just make a mess of it without your guidance. Lead me on, and thanks for helping me. Amen.

it's a roller-coaster LIFE!

HOLD ON! Put up your hands and get ready for the ride of your life. That's right, you're going to experience thrilling highs, crazy lows, and twists and turns like you never imagined. You can close your eyes so you don't know what's coming or scream your lungs out on the big downhill slides or simply hang on for dear life.

Problems, trials, and messes hit everybody. Sometimes you're tuned in to what you did that helped cause them, and other times it all comes out of nowhere. It's not what comes at you that really matters, though. It's the choices you make in handling the big and little messes that make all the difference. The girl who can carefully navigate the hard stuff will find the whole ride more interesting.

Sometimes you stay on track, moving slowly uphill and feeling pretty comfortable about things. You have a moment at the top, and then suddenly you're plunged into a whirlwind of new things, scary things, not-so-certain things. You may wonder if God is still with you in the midst of all those shaky feelings.

The fact is, God is with you always. He isn't just aware of

any problem you may have; he's in the thick of it, ready to help you, holding you up and keeping you close. Don't push God away when troubles hit you. Instead, go to him first, put up your hands, and surrender the moment. Let him know you want and need his help, and he'll be right there beside you.

There's no mess, no part of the ride he can't smooth out. Just trust him with everything you have and all you are.

SCRIPTURE

Although the Lord gives you the bread of adversity and the water of affliction, your teachers will be hidden no more; with your own eyes you will see them. Whether you turn to the right or to the left, your ears will hear a voice behind you, saying, "This is the way; walk in it."

Isaiah 30:20–21

TALK WITH GOD

Lord, I made a big mess of things. I'm not even sure how I got into all this, but I sure need you to help me out. Please be with me today. I put my life in your loving hands. Amen.

how good is YOUR WORD?

REMEMBER WHEN MARY POPPINS talked about a piecrust promise—easily made, easily broken? Which is to say, no promise at all. Yet if promises are meant to be kept, why is it that, more often than not, they're broken? What would we do if God didn't keep his promises?

In Bible times, a promise was a serious matter. When girls got engaged, they were literally promised to their fiancés, and they couldn't get out of the engagement without getting a divorce. A promise had been made, and it was expected to be kept. No exceptions!

Today people take promises lightly—they make piecrust promises. They don't honor the things they say, but they could change all that. You have a chance to change that today. You can decide that you will always be as good as your word. When you make that choice, you'll discover that others will try harder to keep their promises to you as well.

We live in a culture that turns every broken promise into a lawsuit. People don't try to work things out; they simply take the offense as a chance to get even. When you make a promise with your heart, God wants you to honor that promise. You can't run from it or put it off or break it. You can't promise to do better next time with no intention of making an effort. Your promises define your character and tell others who you are.

God keeps his word. He promised to love you and forgive you and bring you back to himself as long as you honor him. You can be sure he'll keep his promise to you. Now what will you do with your promise to him?

SCRIPTURE

It is better not to make a vow than to make one and not fulfill it.

Ecclesiastes 5:5

TALK WITH GOD

Lord, I know I make piecrust promises to you and sometimes to my friends. Help me to really mean what I say and say what I mean so I will always keep my promises. Amen.

ninety-nine and 44/100 percent PURE

MORE THAN 125 YEARS AGO, Proctor & Gamble developed a soap that could float. They claimed the soap called Ivory was 99 and 44/100 percent pure. The soap still makes that claim today, and it still floats. P&G capitalized on purity.

Something that is pure, whether it's pure Ivory, pure gold, or pure soul, stands out and becomes more valuable than other things. Purity, then, isn't something to look at with gloom as though it's a nasty taskmaster. It's something to be acclaimed with joy, something that is close to holiness and floats above the dirt that hugs the earth.

You aren't 100 percent pure on your own; you've been purchased with a great price. Jesus redeemed you so that you could be seen as pure in God's eyes, even more than 99 and 44/100 percent. You are valuable, and the more you can keep from being tainted, tarnished, muddied up by the things of the world, the more your value increases. God wants you to be as holy as you can be so that you can enjoy an even more remarkable relationship with him. After all, he is 100 percent holy, and only he can make you clean.

You may struggle with issues of purity, but when you do, talk about them with God and with someone else you trust, someone who has the wisdom of the Spirit. If it helps, remind yourself that you'd like to be more like Ivory soap, fresh and clean and as pure as you can be. It's a great goal to strive for. When you do fail, remember that God's forgiveness can help you come clean again.

SCRIPTURE

Therefore, since we have these promises, dear friends, let us purify ourselves from everything that contaminates body and spirit, perfecting holiness out of reverence for God.

2 Corinthians 7:1

TALK WITH GOD

Lord, I'm your girl, and I want to be everything you want me to be. Help me make choices that will keep me shining for you in every area of my life. Amen.

turn up
for the
TURNDOWN

NOTHING HURTS LIKE REJECTION! Getting the thick skin that rejection requires isn't easy. Whether you are turned down by your college of choice or rejected by a boyfriend or passed over by the cheerleading squad, it hurts.

The odd part is that much of the time the rejection isn't exactly about you. You can lose a boyfriend who actually thinks you're terrific but just isn't ready for that kind of relationship yet. You can lose an opportunity, maybe to get into a college, because there are just so many applicants and so few openings. Being in the top 10 percent of your class is still an admirable achievement. But this time the school had to draw from certain ethnic cultures or regions of the country or where they had the most scholarship funds. The point is, a lot of rejection happens because of factors that aren't in your control.

Many artists, writers, and sports figures who are well known today experienced a number of rejections before they became household names. Dr. Seuss was turned down by more than forty publishers before he finally brought his

Mulberry Street classic to the world. He had to rise above those rejections and keep trying. He had to turn up again and again with his work in his hand until someone recognized his gifts. You may have to do that too.

Remember you're in excellent company, though. Even Jesus was rejected by the people of his day.

As you face rejection, remember it's only one vote, one step, and if you keep turning up your light, turning up for opportunity, turning up with effort, you'll be able to weather a turndown now and then.

SCRIPTURE

The stone the builders rejected
has become the cornerstone;
the LORD has done this,
and it is marvelous in our eyes.

Psalm 118:22–23

TALK WITH GOD

Lord, I'm suffering over being rejected. Help me to rise above it and keep trying, knowing you're with me and that good things are still in front of me. Amen.

daughter of
THE KING

Do you ever stop to think about what it really means for you to be God's daughter? You're not just on his Christmas-card list, but you're actually family, someone he opens his house and his arms to anytime. You have access to his incredible and never-ending sources for riches, spiritual growth, and love. You're indeed a princess, and that's a wonderful thing.

How does a princess act, then? You could set yourself apart, never give thought to those around you, and just take all the good stuff for yourself. After all, you've been promised a pretty major inheritance. You could try to invite others in so that they can receive some of the inheritance as well.

It's all about your relationship with God. The more you talk with him and build a friendship with him, and the more you seek his advice and comfort, the more you'll have to share with others. God will see to it that you're on top of your game and given all the tools you need to do his work. He'll be a proud Father, and you can be sure he has every intention to give you the kingdom.

It's your job, princess girl, to share with others the love God showers on you. You're his arms and legs, his hands and feet. You're the one he counts on, because your relationship is solid. He loves you beyond measure, and he knows you love him right back. With that kind of love, everything is possible. It's no wonder you're his awesome girl.

SCRIPTURE

May the grace of the Lord Jesus Christ, and the love of God, and the fellowship of the Holy Spirit be with you all.

2 Corinthians 13:14

TALK WITH GOD

Lord, thank you for loving me and taking care of me. Sometimes I really do feel like a princess. I know that everything I have is because of you. Help me to share what you've given me with others. Amen.

your reputation WALKS ahead of you

HENRY HANCOCK SAID, "Out of our beliefs are born deeds; out of our deeds we form habits; out of our habits grows our character; and on our character we build our destiny."

Your character shapes what people think about you. It's what gives you the reputation you have. You're known by the things you do or don't do. Your friend might say, "She always encourages me when I feel down," or another friend might say, "She's just so much fun to be with, and she always lifts my spirits." With those friends you have a fabulous reputation. They no doubt are happy to let others know that you're in their friendship circle.

What happens, though, when your character is trashed by something you do? God gives you choices to make. What if it's easier to go down the wrong road than to take an unpopular direction that would please God? What will you choose?

A reputation is worth protecting. It's one of the reasons actors and sports figures pay PR specialists big bucks to keep their names in or out of the tabloids. They don't want their reputations to get tanked in the press. It's too hard to come back again and rebuild a reputation.

Think of celebrities you've read about who have really ruined their lives by doing things that are clearly wrong. If your life was going to be broadcast in a tabloid today, would you be proud of what you saw in print? Would you feel you had protected your name?

God wants the best from you. He wants you to make choices that reflect your beliefs and values. That's how you build your reputation and create your destiny.

SCRIPTURE

A good name is better than fine perfume.

Ecclesiastes 7:1

TALK WITH GOD

Lord, I've made a few choices I'd hate to see in print. Help me to watch out for myself and stick to my values because I love you. Amen.

R-E-S-P-E-C-T
yourself

YOU'VE BEEN LEARNING ABOUT RESPECT since you were a toddler. Your parents taught you to respect your elders, to be kind to neighbors, to share your toys with others. Respect is a family value, but have you figured out why it's important to you personally and why you want to be respected too?

We often appreciate things that are either ancient or of great value, such as classic writers, poets, and artists of the past. We respect the teachings of Paul or the sermons of Jesus. We respect those who shape the world as we know it.

We also respect those who serve others, like our pastors and youth leaders, the teachers at our school, and the people who keep the streets safe from crime. We respect presidents and leaders of Congress. We generally respect those in authority, especially those who have authority over us and make decisions about our well-being.

Still, these examples might not help us understand why we, too, want to be respected. The US Constitution guards your rights to life, liberty, and the pursuit of happiness, but it doesn't guarantee you respect. You have to earn that. You get people to respect you by the way you act, the way you treat others, and the way you get along in hard times. You become a girl everyone respects when you face life with integrity and honor.

Today, take a good look in the mirror and ask yourself if you respect the girl you see. If you don't, start changing things to make that happen.

SCRIPTURE

Show proper respect to everyone, love the family of believers, fear God, honor the emperor.

1 Peter 2:17

TALK WITH GOD

Lord, I know the people I respect most in the world are my parents and teachers. I want to grow into a woman who is always worthy of their respect and yours. Amen.

salvation: what's the BIG DEAL?

YOU'VE ALREADY GIVEN your heart to Jesus. Whether you did so in recent weeks or when you were just a little girl isn't important; the point is you did it. So what makes that decision such a big one? After all, you could believe in Buddha, but that wouldn't do anything for your salvation. You could believe in Moses, but he didn't die for your sins either. It's your belief in Jesus that has changed everything.

You may wonder if believing in Jesus is a life or death question. Well, the Bible seems to indicate that it is. After all, it's pretty clear we can't believe in anyone else. No other person can do what he did for us — no one else can save us.

You might wonder, too, if being a nice person gets you into heaven. C. S. Lewis said this: "A world of nice people, content in their own niceness, looking no further, turned away from God, would be just as desperately in need of salvation as a miserable world — and might even be more difficult to save."

It's a big deal that you're a believer. It's a great thing that you're a nice person, but the most important thing is that you chose God and he chose you. You can be confident that you'll live this life in his care and under his grace, and then someday you'll go home to his open arms in heaven.

SCRIPTURE

Salvation is found in no one else, for there is no other name under heaven given to mankind by which we must be saved.

Acts 4:12

TALK WITH GOD

Lord, thank you for saving me, for holding me apart so that I can live with you and talk with you right now, and so that someday I'll be home with you in heaven. Amen.

YOU BELONG
to the day!

YOU MAY BE INTRIGUED by the vampire movies, caught momentarily in the things that fantasy projects into the night. You may be in awe of the wizardry of Harry Potter and his friends too. The whole science-fiction/fantasy world is both scary and inviting. It's scary because some of it may remind you of the dark world Satan presides over. Some of it can make you wonder if you're protected when you rise from your bed each morning.

The fact is you are protected because you belong to the day. You're part of the light, and no amount of darkness can snuff it out. In fact, sometimes your light gets brighter when you stand in the dark. What you do, what you choose, is all a matter of self-control.

Have you ever witnessed one of your friends acting out? Did you find it a bit frightening? The only real freedom comes from knowing the boundaries, knowing the playing field. When you don't know where you're going, it doesn't matter when you get there. The same is true of being in control of yourself. If you don't know your own boundaries, if you don't know who you are, then it might not matter how you get through the day. The fact is, you know who you are because you defined your boundaries through your faith in Jesus. You're a Jesus girl.

Self-control is a gift of the Spirit, and it will give you a great chance for a successful life. It will help to keep you healthy and strong.

SCRIPTURE

Since we belong to the day, let us be sober, putting on faith and love as a breastplate, and the hope of salvation as a helmet.   *I Thessalonians 5:8*

TALK WITH GOD

Lord, I get nervous when girls act crazy and out of control. Help me to be ready and willing to stand in the light no matter what I'm doing. I want to please you with the things I do. Amen.

hey!
BE YOURSELF!

IT'S GOOD TO KNOW who you are and to have a healthy self-esteem. It's even better to have confidence because you have faith in God and know that he is faithful to his word and will always care for you. Your sense of self is wholesome and good as long as it's humble and authentic. There's only one real you, after all!

One writer gave this advice:

> Be good to yourself—Be happy. Accept yourself—Be graceful. Value yourself—Be joyful. Forgive yourself—Be at peace. Treat yourself well—Be kind. Balance yourself—Be in harmony with others. Bless yourself—Be open to abundance. Trust yourself—Be confident. Love yourself—Be wholehearted. Empower yourself—Be prayerful. Give of yourself—Be generous. Express yourself—Be truthful.[1]

The point is that a lot of different aspects make up the person you are. Your self-esteem shows itself in your behav-

---

1. Adapted from quote on page 925 of *The Encyclopedia of Christian Quotations*. Writer of original quote unknown.

iors, in how you treat your friends and your family, in how you do your schoolwork and how you share what you have. You can be truthful and joyful and real if you know yourself well enough to put your best self out there.

It's always good to be confident and to know the direction you're going. It's even better to continue to build up your faith so it can support you when other things fall down. You'll have days when you're strong and days when you're wondering what's happening and how you got there. But God is always with you, no matter what kind of day you're having. Most of all, he wants the real you to show up.

SCRIPTURE

Do not throw away your confidence; it will be richly rewarded.

Hebrews 10:35

TALK WITH GOD

Lord, help me to have a healthy sense of myself, based on the confidence and the reality of you and the place you hold within my heart. Amen.

serving GOD with joy

IF YOU WERE TO TUNE IN TO A TALK SHOW, you might hear the host give you the top ten reasons why we do something the way we do it. You've seen top-ten lists before. What if you were to hear a description of the top ten reasons to please God? It might sound something like this:

The Top Ten Reasons to Please God
10. He understands you.
9. He knows you.
8. He is honest.
7. He is smart.
6. He is kind.
5. He is generous.
4. He is forgiving.
3. He is always available to you.
2. He loves you. (So much so Jesus gave his life for you.)
1. He rewards you with eternal life.

There are a lot more than ten reasons to please your Father in heaven, so it might be fun to make your own top-ten list. God watches out for you, protects you, and gives you guidance every day. He wants you to be available and dependable so that you're ready to serve. If you are, then he can do a lot of things for the good of others through you. If you're not available, then he has to find someone else.

Show God exactly who you are, and let him know you're ready and willing to be of service. After all, the greatest reward of serving others is the deep satisfaction that grows in your heart. Give yourself ten good reasons to serve everyone with joy and love.

SCRIPTURE

Therefore, my dear brothers and sisters, stand firm. Let nothing move you. Always give yourselves fully to the work of the Lord, because you know that your labor in the Lord is not in vain.

I Corinthians 15:58

TALK WITH GOD

Lord, I do want to please you every day, and I want to be of service in any way I can. Thanks for loving me far more than the top ten reasons I have to please you. Amen.

facing
your own
GOLIATH

IMAGINE THAT ON YOUR WAY TO SCHOOL TODAY, you come across a man who is over nine feet tall. Not only that, but he's shouting nasty remarks as people pass by, ensuring that no one comes close to him. He's an oversized bully, and his name is "shyness." After all, shyness feels like a giant problem.

Some girls are pretty shy. They're not only shy about making friends and meeting boys, but they're shy about life in general. They certainly don't like getting up in front of the class to speak, or having to lead a group activity at youth camp. They would much rather recede into the background.

If you're a shy girl, then you have to find a way to face your own giant, the one you created. You learned to be shy; you weren't born that way. You stopped believing in your own power, your own ability to please those around you. You lost your confidence, and it's time to get it back.

David took five smooth stones with him when he faced Goliath. You might need some smooth stones of your own. One stone might remind you that God made you with a strong spirit. He gave you a firm foundation and all the tools you need to be successful in the world. One stone might be forgiveness. God forgave all your sins so you don't need to carry any burden of guilt. Another stone might be forgetfulness. Maybe you need to forget the things that prevent you from meeting others. Forget that you don't think you're good enough. Forget that you don't think you have anything to offer. Go ahead, give one of those stones a shot. It's time to drop the giant of shyness today. You've got friends to make and a world of wonderful things to explore.

SCRIPTURE

For the Spirit God gave us does not make us timid, but gives us power, love and self-discipline.   2 Timothy 1:7

TALK WITH GOD

Lord, I'm shy, and I don't like it. I run away from things sometimes just because I'm too afraid to step out and take a chance. Please help me knock this Goliath in the head. Amen.

sisters, sisters, ever-devoted SISTERS

YOU MAY NOT FEEL THIS WAY RIGHT NOW, but it's possible that you and your sisters or brothers will grow up to be best friends. Oh, sure, you're scrapping a bit now, but you won't always have a relationship like that. And you can learn from each others' differences as well.

The New Testament tells about some friends of Jesus who were sisters. Their names were Mary and Martha. They were adults who shared the responsibilities of running a household, and the disciples often met at their house. Martha was always gracious and hospitable, tending to the needs of her guests, making sure they had snacks and goodies to nibble. Mary didn't do the hostess thing because she preferred to listen to the news of the day and to sit at Jesus's feet as he shared information about God. As you can imagine, Martha wasn't thrilled with this arrangement. After all, she wanted to go sit and listen, but she had work to do. She thought Mary should be helping her.

Things finally blew up, and Martha was miffed at Mary. She complained to Jesus in the same way you might complain to your parents over your sister or brother not helping you do the chores. To Martha's surprise, Jesus said the best thing Mary could do was to sit at his feet and listen to him. Sometimes we can learn important things from our siblings. God created us all a bit differently so that we could understand more fully how valuable each one of us is to his plan for the world. Mary and Martha learned to cooperate and get along. You may be learning that lesson too.

Siblings are special. No one else will know your family history or love you the same way. Today and always, thank God for the special people he put in your life. Thank him for your siblings.

SCRIPTURE

Take a look at Mary and Martha's story in Luke 10:38–42.

TALK WITH GOD

Lord, sometimes I don't understand why my brother picks on me or why my sister doesn't help more with the chores. Help me to love them the way you love them. Amen.

running a few MORE LAPS

IF YOU'RE INTO SPORTS AT ALL, you know that some activities take a lot of strength. You can't really run without developing the muscles in your legs. You can't swim laps without strong arm and stomach muscles. If you're a dancer, you strengthen nearly every part of your body. It's great to be strong and in good physical shape.

What does it mean, though, to be strong in the Lord—to grow into a strong woman? You need inner strength. You need the kind of strength that comes from a relationship so tied into Jesus that you can do anything through him. You need to have a foundation under your feet.

Think about some of the strong women you know. Maybe you think your mother is a strong woman, or your aunt. Maybe you think of Mother Teresa or Maya Angelou or some current Bible teachers like Joyce Meyer or Beth Moore. Were they born strong, or did they grow strong?

Inner strength is developed in a similar way to physical strength. It takes time and practice. It takes devotion and intention. You have to want to get more, and you have to give more. When you start the day with prayer, take time to read your Bible, build in time to journal or meditate quietly, you flex your inner spiritual muscles. It won't be long before those practices will be a daily part of you because you won't feel like you've exercised your ability to connect with God without them.

Remember to take the time to strengthen who you are in Jesus.

SCRIPTURE

Have I not commanded you? Be strong and courageous. Do not be afraid; do not be discouraged, for the LORD your God will be with you wherever you go.

Joshua 1:9

TALK WITH GOD

Lord, help me to become stronger in you every day. Help me to want to practice hard to gain the strength only you can give me. Amen.

loosening
THE TENSION

STRESS IS A FACT OF LIFE, and being a teenager doesn't make it any easier. After all, you have a ton of schoolwork, a slew of extracurricular activities, expectations from your family to behave in a certain way, chores to do, youth group to attend, and God to figure out. You also have a wide variety of friends to deal with, and some of them take a lot of hand holding. It's no wonder you're freaked out. It all feels like a mess!

So what can you do when you realize that all the angst you feel isn't going to let go of you easily? It knocks you a little off center, makes you slightly moody, and perhaps causes you to feel disconnected from God. What can God do about all this stuff anyway?

The fact is, God is still your go-to guy. He's still the One who can calm your fears, carry your burdens, and help you manage the overloaded and overwhelmed feelings you have. Praying is one of the best things you can do when you feel this way. Another helpful tool is to journal the events and your feelings.

Pray, journal, take intentional breaks to chat with friends, and let your parents know what's going on. They may negotiate some of the chores with you if you let them in on your freaky workload. They may even give you a pass to not do a few things just now.

Before angst becomes a regular inhabitant of your space, try some of these things to lighten the mood. Look for the window of opportunity for things to change. If you see that things may settle down in ten days, then work hard and breathe a sigh of relief when life get back to normal . . . whatever that is!

SCRIPTURE

Do not be anxious about anything, but in every situation, by prayer and petition, with thanksgiving, present your requests to God.   *Philippians 4:6*

TALK WITH GOD

Lord, I'm overwhelmed with my life right now. Please remind me of the things I can do to lighten my load a bit. Thanks for watching out for me ... Always! Amen.

living well is BETTER than living it up

SOMETIMES WE ADMIRE OTHER GIRLS for the wrong reasons. We see the popular girls getting lots of dates, going to parties, hanging with a wide variety of friends, and somehow never seeming to struggle. It looks as if they have life on a silver platter, and nobody even told you that was an option. They're living it up, and from where you stand, that looks good!

The thing is, it looks good, but who knows if it really is good? What God has in mind for you is that you would live well and find success in your own way. His view of success is very different from the one the world keeps putting in front of your face. It's a success that depends a lot on your heart and how tuned in you are to God.

The poet Elisabeth-Anne "Bessie" Anderson had this to say about success:

> That person is a success who has lived well, laughed often
> and loved much;
> Who has enjoyed [...] the respect of intelligent men and the
> love of little children;
> Who has filled his niche and accomplished his task;

Who never lacked appreciation for earth's beauty or failed to
   express it;
Who has left the world better than he found it,
Whether an improved poppy, a perfect poem, or a rescued
   soul;
Who looked for the best in others and gave the best he had.

Make it your plan to live well—in a way that pleases
God—and then you can live it up for all the right reasons.
You may find that success is all around you and the grace of
God is with you. You are meant to succeed.

SCRIPTURE

I have fought the good fight, I have
finished the race, I have kept the faith.

2 Timothy 4:7

TALK WITH GOD

Lord, I admit that sometimes I think
other girls are having more fun than I
am, and I start to convince myself that
they must be smarter too. Help me to
live well—in a way that will help me
leave the world a better place than I
found it. Amen.

who will dry THEIR TEARS?

IF YOU REMEMBER HURRICANE KATRINA, which did so much damage in New Orleans back in 2005, or you've witnessed the devastation of a tsunami or an earthquake, you're familiar with the suffering that goes on worldwide. Missionaries all over the world work tirelessly to help in any way they can when these huge "acts of God" happen.

Suffering has always been a part of life. We've been given a wide range of emotions, and we can't help feeling sadness when bad things happen. We hurt with those far and near who have needs way beyond what we can understand. We recognize that we live in a world with a lot of differences. Some people have no drinking water or food; some people have access to more than they will ever need.

As you look at your own life and the things you've suffered, it might help to remind yourself of what God *has* given you. He has probably provided you with everything you need to sustain a healthy life and to grow happily.

What can you do, though, when someone you love is suffering, or when you see the monumental troubles around the world? Today, with the Internet, you can see just about everything that happens in the world. You can see bombs dropping on innocent people. You can see babies starving and children with no parents.

What you can do is pray. Pray today for everyone who is suffering. If you can, organize your youth group to help manage a current problem. If you become overwhelmed by these things, talk to your pastor, your parents, and your heavenly Father about them. Do what you can to relieve the suffering of one other person today, and dry a few tears.

SCRIPTURE

We boast in the hope of the glory of God. Not only so, but we also glory in our sufferings, because we know that suffering produces perseverance; perseverance, character; and character, hope.

Romans 5:2–4

TALK WITH GOD

Lord, I can't understand all the suffering that I read or hear about, either in the world or right in my own school and community. Please help all the people who suffer, and help me to remember to pray more intentionally for them. Amen.

broken hearts, broken LIVES

TEEN SUICIDE RATES ARE ESCALATING. Some teens decide they can't take it anymore when a bully makes their life miserable. Some get discouraged, convinced that their dreams will never come true; and some worry that love has passed them by after they go through a serious breakup.

The Spirit of God grieves for the brokenhearted teens who believe they no longer have a reason to live. Life can be tough, there's no question. It can even seem too dark to find just a flicker of light, but the truth is, with a little time, things will change. Tomorrow often brings new opportunity and new hope. It's just a matter of holding on.

Whew! What kind of belief convinces teens that they are no longer worthy of life? What kind of brokenness is too damaged for God to fix? The answer truly is this: God can heal brokenness. Period. Sure, it probably won't happen today or tomorrow. But it will happen. When you come to him, doubtful, heavyhearted, feeling like you just want to give up, then he can help. Give up! Give up the burden and let him carry it for you. Give up the anxiety and the stories in your head that keep you confused and broken.

If you or someone you know is even remotely considering suicide, don't hesitate to get help. There is help. Jesus opens his arms to you, and he has a plan for you, for your good. Give him a chance to show you what it is. Talk to your pastor, a counselor, or a teacher, but talk to somebody.

Your heart may be broken, but it will mend. God promises to help you.

SCRIPTURE

Cast your cares on the LORD
   and he will sustain you;
he will never let
   the righteous be shaken.

Psalm 55:22

TALK WITH GOD

Lord, I pray for wholeness, for victory over depression, for strength in you. I pray for my friends too, who suffer with broken hearts and broken spirits. Amen.

glorious GIFTS

SOME TALENTS ARE OBVIOUS. You may be a strong diver, and even though you've never had a lesson, you know instinctively what to do and how to perfect the art form. You may have an ear for foreign language and be able to pick up a new language fairly quickly once you're immersed in it. You may simply be the kind of networker who knows how to get people together and how to get them to volunteer their time and services for a local fund-raiser.

Whatever they are, you can probably name your talents. But if you think you can simply count them on one hand, you may not be looking hard enough to see what they are. You have a lot of gifts, and God wants you to explore them and use them for his glory.

Hidden talents often emerge by accident. Maybe the foreign-language class is full, so you take sign language instead. Voilà! You discover that you're not only a natural signer, but you love it too. Or perhaps you get a chance to go on a mission trip to Turkey, and you discover that you have a knack for working with people in other cultures. Sometimes you discover a talent just by trying something new.

You may wonder why God moves you around or encourages you to change things up a bit. He wants you to try things you haven't tried before. You might benefit his people if you grasp the talent you didn't even know you had and do something with it. As you look at what you already do and what you already know, see if you can uncover a new talent, a gift you didn't even know was there.

SCRIPTURE
There are different kinds of gifts, but the same Spirit distributes them.
1 Corinthians 12:4

TALK WITH GOD
Lord, thank you for the talents you've given me. Some of them don't seem so special, but I'm happy you've given them to me anyway. Help me discover what else you have for me, and help me not to be afraid to try new things. Amen.

TEMPTING,
very tempting ...

SHOPLIFTING IS TEMPTING. Sometimes it's tempting because the retail outlet makes it so easy to walk off with the merchandise. Sometimes it's tempting because your friends do it and have gotten away with it, so why wouldn't you? After all, they don't take big things, just a T-shirt now and then, or an eye shadow at Walgreens. Everybody does it, so it's no big deal, right?

Don't be fooled. Everybody is tempted, from the guy who fudges on his taxes and doesn't report his full income to the woman who steals away for a banana split after she's tried for weeks to lose weight. Temptations are there, but they don't have to win.

In his first letter to the Corinthians, Paul said that with every temptation, God provides a way out. The trouble is, too often we don't look for the escape hatch. The problem is us, then, because we cave in too quickly.

Thomas à Kempis said, "By little and little, and by patience with long-suffering through God's help, [you will] more easily overcome [temptations] than with violence and [your own power]." In other words, you may resist temptation on your own, but you'll do it a lot better with God's help.

When the Devil tempted Jesus, he tried to do so with food, because Jesus was starving after fasting for forty days. Jesus had to recite from Scripture to get the Devil to flee, and you may have to do the same thing.

Be ready to face temptations for what they are, and remind the tempter you're a daughter of God and you have no intention of giving in.

SCRIPTURE

No temptation has overtaken you except what is common to mankind. And God is faithful; he will not let you be tempted beyond what you can bear. But when you are tempted, he will also provide a way out so that you can endure it.

1 Corinthians 10:13

TALK WITH GOD

Lord, please help me resist the temptations that pop into my life. It's so easy sometimes to give in to cheating on a test or stealing little things from a dollar store. Help me to find a way out of any temptations that come my way. Amen.

can you trust ANYBODY these days?

TAKE A TRUST WALK WITH A FRIEND. You're blindfolded or have your eyes closed, and your friend is the guide. Your guide talks to you and tells you where to step and where to turn. You have to trust that your guide will keep you safe and not let you walk into the street or fall over a trash can. Even with the best intentions, it is hard for someone to guide you, so you need to choose your guide wisely.

Sometimes figuring out who to trust is tricky. Even some adults can prove to be unreliable. It's important that others earn your trust and that you don't just hand it over. Be on your guard and ask God to help you know who you can really trust.

Here's what Francis de Sales said about trust:

Do not look forward to the changes and chances of this life in fear; rather look to them with full hope that, as they arise, God, whose you are, will deliver you out of them. He is your keeper. He has kept you from the day you were born. If you hold fast to his dear hand, he will lead you safely through all things; and, when you cannot stand, he will bear you in his arms. Do not worry about what may happen tomorrow. Our father will either shield you from suffering, or he will give you strength to bear it.

Trust in God, then, for he will always be beside you. He has already earned your trust.

SCRIPTURE

The LORD is my shepherd, I lack nothing.
  He makes me lie down in green
    pastures,
he leads me beside quiet waters,
  he refreshes my soul.
He guides me along the right paths
  for his name's sake.
Even though I walk
  through the darkest valley,
I will fear no evil,
  for you are with me.   Psalm 23:1–4

TALK WITH GOD

Lord, thank you for guiding me and protecting me. Thank you for being so trustworthy. Help me to be the kind of girl that other people can trust. Amen.

worry and faith
CAN'T DANCE

SOMEBODY ONCE SAID that "today is the tomorrow we worried about yesterday." Does that ring a bell with you? Can you look back and think of things you worried about last year, or last semester, or even last week, that are already looking different now? No doubt you can, because it's part of human nature to worry.

The good news is that girls with faith do have another option. You can take your worries and hand them right over to God. You don't even have to hold them for a moment if you don't want to. He's ready to take them on.

The thing is that worry and faith don't dance together well. When faith is in the lead, worry almost disappears. When worry is in the lead, faith wonders what happened. It's not a pretty sight.

Sometimes it helps to write your worries on little strips of paper; then one by one pray about them, hand them to God, and burn the paper. Then you don't have the worry in your hand anymore. It's a helpful exercise if you find that a particular worry keeps leaping up, demanding attention.

Joyce Meyer talks a lot about the idea that what we think about matters. She says we need to think about what we're thinking about. If we've gone off on a worry crusade and let a whole army of worries gang up on us, it's not going to be easy to win the battle. If we stop and realize that we're worrying instead of giving God the chance to take on the problem, it might make us think twice.

One thing to remember is that if you have a worry, pray about it and give it to God before you go to bed. After all, he'll be up all night anyhow.

SCRIPTURE

Therefore do not worry about tomorrow, for tomorrow will worry about itself. Each day has enough trouble of its own.

Matthew 6:34

TALK WITH GOD

Lord, I keep trying to invite worry to dance with me, but I know that's not a good idea. Please give me the faith I need to let go of the worry and just put it in your mighty hands. Amen.

NIV True Images: The Bible for Teen Girls

NIV True Images, the only NIV Bible designed specifically for teen girls ages 13 – 16, is for real teenage girls with real lives. Packed with edgy graphics, personal notes, cool quizzes, challenging insights, and open discussion about the realities of life, this Bible is designed to help you build a closer relationship with God. *NIV True Images* is as sincere about your walk with God as you are, helping you discover his will for all areas of your life, including relating to your family, dealing with friends, work, sports, guys, and so much more.

Whether you are reading the reality-based "In Focus" stories about real teenage issues, drawing encouragement from "Love Notes From God," or letting "Truth or Dare" challenge you in practical ways, what you will value most is discovering how deeply God is involved in your life: laughing when you laugh; grieving over your tears; listening when no one else seems to care; smiling because you delight him; and loving you through thick and thin.

Available in stores and online!

Made to Crave for Young Women

Satisfying Your Deepest Desires with God

Lysa TerKeurst, President of Proverbs 31 Ministries, and Shaunti Feldhahn, bestselling social researcher

What's the last thing you really craved?

New shoes, a decadent dessert, popularity, a date with that cute guy in English ... every day is filled with things we want and crave. Things that will make us happy, at least for a moment. But what happens when that moment is gone and the crave returns?

There's often nothing wrong with wanting certain things, but God didn't create us to be consumed by earthly cravings. He created us to crave Him, and a happiness that lasts. In this teen adaptation of the bestselling *Made to Crave*, the deep emotional, physical, and material cravings you face are explored—desires that can turn into spending too much, over or under eating, needing a boyfriend, or more. Though real-life stories and support from people who have been where you are, you will also discover how to truly crave God and the love and comfort He wants us to have, and how craving heavenly things can make the earthly cravings easier to overcome.

You were made to crave more than this world has to offer.

Available in stores and online!

ZONDERVAN®
.com

Talk It Up!

Want free books?
First looks at the best new fiction?
Awesome exclusive merchandise?

We want to hear from you!

Give us your opinions on titles, covers, and stories.
Join the Z Street Team.

Email us at zstreetteam@zondervan.com
to sign up today!

Also—Friend us on Facebook!

www.facebook.com/goodteenreads

- Video Trailers
- Connect with your favorite authors
- Sneak peeks at new releases
- Giveaways
- Fun discussions
- And much more!